# YARDBIRD USA

How the United States Became
the World's Leading Jailer
(Musings of a Trial Lawyer)

Jack W. Cline

Strategic Book Publishing and Rights Co.

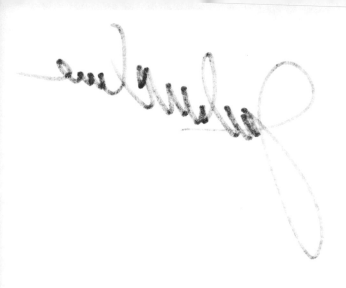

Strategic Book Publishing and Rights Co.
12620 FM 1960, Suite A4-507
Houston, TX 77065
www.sbpra.com

ISBN:978-1-61204-594-8

Book Design: Suzanne Kelly

# About the Author

Jack William Cline was born and resides in Grove City, Pennsylvania. He graduated from Allegheny College, B.S. cum laude in 1981 with a double major in Economics and History. He was an All-American in Golf. He obtained his Juris Doctor degree in 1984 from the University of Pittsburgh School of Law and was winner of the FIC National Writing Contest that year. He was admitted to practice law in the Commonwealth of Pennsylvania and the United States District Court in Western Pennsylvania in 1984, where he continues to practice with the firm of Stranahan, Stranahan & Cline. Attorney Cline represents individuals charged with crimes, as well as individuals and businesses faced with government regulatory and administrative actions. He has handled over 125 jury trials throughout Western Pennsylvania and has handled over two thousand criminal and traffic offenses in his career. He is a President's Club Member of the Pennsylvania Association of Criminal Defense Lawyers (PACDL), a member of the National Association of Criminal Defense Lawyers (NACDL) and a member of the

Mercer County, Allegheny County, and Pennsylvania Bar Associations. In 2003, Mr. Cline was selected and served on President George W. Bush's National Republican Congressional Committee as co-chairman of Business Advisory Council, after which he resigned as a Republican and joined the Libertarian Party.

# Dedication

This book is dedicated to my parents, Jack Z. and Shirley Cline. Along with all of the other things they have done for me over the years, they sent me to Allegheny College, a classic liberal arts school located in the snow belt of North-western Pennsylvania. Although Allegheny had us trapped for four long years, they did not spoon-feed us there. Instead our professors gave us the tools to acquire the knowledge we needed and desired, and they challenged us to think and write in a critical and independent fashion. This is a skill that has inspired me in my career and in life. Thanks to my parents and to Old Allegheny.

# Table of Contents

Jack W. Cline

# Introduction

We in the United States love to hear ourselves say that we are the greatest nation on Earth. But it is time to acknowledge that we have serious problems that are deeply rooted in our past. The United States of America has a sad history of enslaving and imprisoning its own people, and has only stubbornly relinquished each and every opportunity to exploit and enslave our fellow man.

In Europe, slavery was abolished and relegated to colonial possessions way back during the Enlightenment. Even in most European Colonies, slavery was abolished by the middle of the eighteenth century. For example, Great Britain abolished the ownership of slaves in 1772, before we had even declared independence. Slave trade was abolished by 1807 and was prohibited in all colonies by 1833, some three decades before the slavery issue led to a Civil War here in the United States[1].

Most of our early presidents were slave masters, including Thomas Jefferson, the architect of our republic and one of the most prolific and articulate proponents of personal liberty in the history of the world. Jefferson owned 267 slaves by 1822 and freed only three, plus five more at his death that were all blood relatives[2]. Slavery was not abolished in this country until the emancipation proclamation

---

1 Davies, Norman: *Europe History*, Harper Perennial 1998, 166-167.
2 Loewen, James W.: *Lies My Teacher Told Me*, Simon & Schuster 1995, 148

on the trail of a bloody Civil War, less than 150 years ago, and its abolition was "to save the union," not a moral proclamation. Lincoln himself stated that he had no intention that the proclamation would actually permit the Negro to vote or sit as a juror[3].

The enslavement of the African American until political expediency dictated otherwise is a stain on our country, which may be surpassed only by our treatment of the Native American "Indian." Indians begged to be included in the Republic, and after being turned down, begged to have their own Indian State. Even after they adopted the settlers' way of life, such as slave ownership, the Indians were exploited. The United States government "purchased" their land from France and Spain, and later, with the help of the "Indian Removal" statutes, deported them from their property as if they were herds of animals. The passion of President Andrew Jackson was this "Indian Removal," which required him to welsh on treaties and encourage southern states to ignore federal law and half-assed Supreme Court decisions on the subject. The approach that this era's leaders of the United States maintained towards the American Indian is a shame to any citizen of this country[4].

Even in the middle of the twentieth century, when at war with Japan, we herded up completely innocent American citizens with one-sixteenth or more Japanese heritage and incarcerated them in concentration camps, conduct different only in quantity, not in principle, from those of our Allies (e.g., Soviet Russia) and our enemy, Nazi Germany. It was, by all accounts, an unjustified and wretched feat for a nation founded on individual freedom and liberty, embracing all nationalities and races as the world's "melt-

3 Loewen, James W.: *Lies My Teacher Told Me*, Simon & Schuster 1995, 155
4 Howe, Daniel Walker: *What Hath God Wrought: The Transformation of America 1815-1848*, pp. 328-366, Oxford University Press, 2007

ing pot." Unfortunately, we have continued in this vein in many respects.

In the 1980s and carrying on into the twenty-first century, our modern brand of slavery has taken the form of a prison society. We have increased the rate at which we are imprisoning our own people at a breakneck speed. The United States of America's use of imprisonment has surpassed every other nation on earth, and must appear to other civilized (and uncivilized) societies as almost fetishistic.

The statistics are mind-boggling and will be illustrated and discussed in more detail. They are necessary in order to appreciate the scope of the fetish.

For starters, we top the world's list with 2.29 million prisoners, followed distantly by Red China (1.57 million) and post-Soviet Russia (890,000). Yes, we have two and a half times as many people in our jails as the Russians do (King's College London, International Centre for Prison Studies, Jan. 29, 2009 report). It is fortunate that reliable statistics for imprisonment rates in Russia under the totalitarian regime of Joe Stalin are not available. Such statistics could create quite an embarrassing comparison for us in the "land of the free."

On a basis of prisoners per one hundred thousand inhabitants, we blow everyone out of the water. The United States of America has 756 per one hundred thousand citizens locked up compared to the world average of 153. Other diverse nations such as Belgium, Austria, Germany, Iraq, Italy, Japan, Finland, Croatia, Egypt, Madagascar, Bolivia, Venezuela, among many others, imprison less than one hundred people per one hundred thousand, that is to say less than one-eighth of our imprisonment rate.

These statistics do not include the hundreds of thousands of juveniles being detained as delinquents in juvenile facilities. Fortunately, such figures are difficult to obtain due to the confidentiality maintained by some jurisdictions over juvenile records.

We in the United States have either developed the most diabolical population of miscreants in the world, or we have allowed our legal/political system to run off the tracks. Hopefully it will soon become clear that the problem is, in fact, with our system, and unfortunately the problem is a profound one in need of immediate attention.

Our bursting prisons are the result of the Judicial Branch giving way to the Legislative (political) branch, giving up a fundamental prerogative to exercise judicial discretion in the imposition of sentences for criminal defendants. The Legislatures have been permitted to establish not only mandatory sentences for various offenses, but sentence guidelines to cover virtually every criminal case. The Legislatures have also seen fit to enact laws criminalizing almost every act viewed as unmannerly by a Quaker Sabbath School teacher, and the Judiciary has failed to strike down any significant portion of the sentencing mandates or the criminal statutes. In fact, the Judiciary has scarcely taken umbrage to this arrant infringement. How and why did the Judiciary geld itself? What has occurred to our prison population over the past quarter-century as a result? How can the spiral be reversed?

We are in the midst of a crisis. In fact, it has already become evident in California, Indiana, Pennsylvania, and New Jersey to name a few states. The form of the crisis is, of course, financial. As states begin to collapse under their own weight, squealing for federal bailout monies, it will become clear that a big part of the states' financial woes are its misuse and overuse of the incredibly expensive calaboose.

A financial crisis always becomes a political crisis, since the legislative branch controls public finance. That makes the scenario all the more dangerous. Allowing the legislatures to attempt to "correct" the prison population blowout as they face budgetary meltdowns will invite more debacle. State legislatures in this situation will protect their state workers' pensions and other pet projects and will be backed into a forced reduction of prison costs. Releasing prisoners is the ticket and this will be done in the most politically expedient fashion, the same manner that the prisons were filled up in times that the state coffers were flush with monies from an expanding economy. The only thing in the criminal justice system that could be worse than allowing legislative control over who goes to jail is allowing legislative control over who gets out. The possibilities for abuse, malfeasance, cronyism, and skullduggery are almost mind-blowing.

The decision on who goes to jail and for how long must be returned entirely to the judiciary. This is the correct solution, and this will take some effort and fortitude on the part of this timorous branch of government. Hopefully, the judiciary has not emaciated itself to the extent that it cannot re-assume this crucial role in our society.

■

Most materials written about prison overcrowding are either (a) sterile, statistical recitations with no worthwhile analysis as to how or why the problem has occurred, or (b) budget crisis and alarm scenarios for states and municipalities trying to find a way to pay for their bloated prison systems, or (c) amateurish diatribes by NAACP or ACLU type organizations railing about prison conditions. Nothing I have seen actually views the effect of our political tinkering in the judicial system from the dirt up, from the prospective of individuals run through the system and who have been irreparably damaged by it[5].

---

5 One Exception. Judge Jeffrey K. Sprecher, also from Pennsylvania, has just written: *Justice or Just This? A Constitutional Trespass.* This book analyses the political takeover of sentencing from the perspective of a Judge of nearly twenty years'

In this brilliant and remarkable study, I have carefully chosen a dozen criminal cases that played out over the past five years throughout Western Pennsylvania. In all but one of these cases I was the defense lawyer. Each case was picked to illustrate a particular point, all hopefully leading to the same general conclusion. The cases are all factually accurate. There is no need to fudge such things and most of them would be impossible to fictionalize. All cases can be documented by reference to the case files as cited. Only certain names have been altered in order to avoid embarrassment, protect innocent persons, and to avoid the unnecessary identification of imbeciles.

My travails through the criminal justice system have now surpassed a quarter-century. I have handled well over two thousand separate cases, along with several hundred civil cases. Not a single one of these cases have ended without someone being dissatisfied. For anyone seeking a career as a trial lawyer, the most important advice I can offer is that you must be able to deal with, and even enjoy, conflict. The day to day practice of criminal defense law, if done in earnest, is bloody trench warfare, a constant battle with witnesses, prosecutors, police, judges, bureaucrats, and, at times, one's own client. Where a doctor or dentist can work for a common goal for the patient and his family—health and comfort—the lawyer can only make his client healthy and comfortable by making the other party uncomfortable and miserable.

There must be a winner and loser in the law and in this respect it is much more akin to a sport or a war than a profession. As one of my professors from the University

---

experience. Although the book was still in print as of this writing, I believe it will be an excellent study. I was able to meet Judge Sprecher at a PACDL conference in the spring of 2011, and his frustration over the present state of affairs was manifest. It actually led him to write the book and publish it himself.

of Pittsburgh School of Law told us in our first year, "As lawyers you will hear your clients tell you they 'did not do nothing wrong. Get me out of this and don't send me a big bill.' Whereas the patient tells the physician, 'Thanks, Doc, you're the best for pulling me through this.' Get used to this dichotomy," he advised, "and if you can't handle it, go up the hill (to the medical school) and push pills." It's a comment I heard in 1981 and have never forgotten.

Trial law leads to unmatched acrimony. After one trial I was nearly run over by the vehicle of the mother of an enraged witness when crossing the street to my office, immediately after the verdict and in broad daylight. This woman was not even a witness or a party to the case, but as a family member of a party, she had worked herself into an uncontrollable rage. Only a last-minute leap by sheer instinct saved me from a horrible thumping. Another time I was plagued by a series of clandestine death threats. An anonymous person made calls to my office, announcing to the receptionist that "Cline was a dead man," and then the threats escalated, saying that he would be waiting inside my house at night. At that time I lived alone in a small ranch house on the south side of Grove City, and for several days when I got home after work, I would check all the closets and other hiding areas, gripping a five iron in my right hand. I doubt that an orthodontist has ever had to endure this inconvenience. (Later this scorned freak identified himself and apologized to me. The case involved $2,250.)

An even punier amount of money created an open sore with a client for whom I successfully obtained an expungement of his criminal record. I charged a measly $250 for this service at the time (additional red tape now required for this procedure has nearly doubled the cost). This amount included the court filing fees and expungement costs, which varied from case to case. After the expungement was already done, the client's check bounced. Not only was I out my fee, but also the expenses I had advanced on his behalf. I wrote him and achieved no result, so I sent him the obligatory letter that a bad check charge may ensue if he did not make his check good in ten days. He called in a rage, stating that he would never do business with me again. It would have been tempting to repeat the story about David Letterman's overnight visit to the Clinton White House during Slick Willie's presidency. Clinton, upon catching Letterman coming out of Hillary's bedroom, warned Letterman: "I'll have no more of that!"—whereupon Letterman retorted: "Neither will I!"

Most of us have been called almost every name imaginable to the uneducated. The threats (seldom carried out) are in many ways less egregious than the blizzard of slanderous terms assigned to our profession. Once, after a silly summary traffic trial in Butler County where I cross-examined the other driver (a motorcyclist) on failing to have his headlights on, I was rushed after court by the cyclist's enraged wife in the hallway. "You are a cock sucker," she frothed. "Hush," I pleaded, "Don't tell everyone; I'm trying to quit."

But the experience of a trial lawyer should be respected and never underestimated. A criminal defense lawyer must be able to handle constant friction, animosity, disappointment, defeat. A trial lawyer must be able to sift through a blizzard of information. He or she is typically bombarded with facts from the police reports, the client, and the witnesses, yet some of the most important and helpful information must be culled from difficult and reluctant sources. The trial lawyer must decide what is wheat and what is chaff and on short notice present the worthwhile kernels in the form of precise and carefully worded questions that would overcome objections from the opponent and the Judge. The trial lawyer must be able to relate to the lowliest dirt bag in town and in the same case be able to cross-examine an expert chemist, radiologist, or criminal investigator. The skills and perspective developed by trial lawyers create for them a unique perspective on people and the system that they operate in.

The cases I have chosen are specifically intended to illustrate aspects of our criminal justice system, mainly relative to sentencing, which have led to the United States being the world's most prolific jail house nation. Naturally, many of these cases have resulted in my clients being imprisoned. Although I would rather crow about the cases I have won and instances where my clients have walked out of court free, those cases do not show the effect on real people of our criminal justice system warped by politics, and even though each of the cases I discuss here are unique and bizarre in their own way, there is no doubt that they are being paralleled throughout the state and the nation on a daily basis, delivering the United States of America the title of *Yardbird USA*.

It is my goal and hope that you will enjoy reading about the cases and your intellect will be challenged by their implications. And hopefully you will come away with your own opinion, one way or another, on whether our system has been warped and perhaps what might be done before mistakes are compounded into disaster.

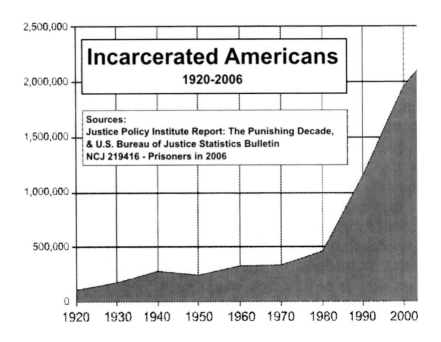

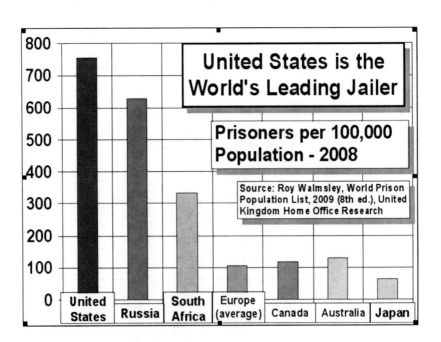

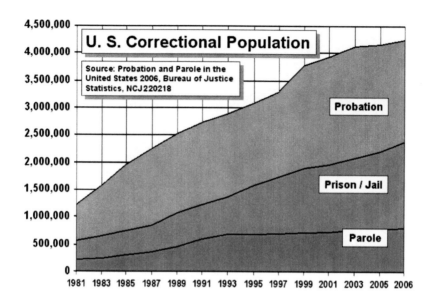

# YARDBIRD USA

# CHAPTER 1

# The Ghetto

If the experience in U.S. prisons was truly "correction"—melding punishment, recompense, and rehabilitation—then the United States holding the world title as the most prolific jailer may not be such an embarrassing distinction.

In fact, however, it is quite the opposite. The jail is a ghetto walled in concrete. The setting is rancid. If one would not be a criminal going into prison, it's a good chance he or she would come out as one.

At least in the real ghetto the playing field is more level. In the street ghetto, the most motivated, the most powerful, and the most cunning hooligans prevail. In the prisons, the dice are loaded. Jail turnkeys are able to exploit their unique positions to blackmail their prey. They can provide contraband that is banned in prisons, from heroin to cell phones, in order to satisfy their prurient self-interests. No matter how stupid they are, the guards have the clear advantage: utilizing the stick—dual threats of continued incarceration or parole denials—along with the carrot—usually sexual favors. The message supplied to prisoners is hardly one of rehabilitation, respect for authority, or obedience to the law.

Apparently, those persons with sadistic tendencies are attracted to the career of prison corrections. Charles A.

Graner, Jr. (born 1968) is a former U.S. Army reservist who was convicted of prisoner abuse in connection with the 2003–2004 Abu Ghraib prisoner abuse scandal. Graner, with other soldiers from his unit, the 372nd Military Police Company, was accused of allowing and inflicting sexual, physical, and psychological abuse of Iraqi prisoners of war in Abu Ghraib, a notorious prison in Baghdad during the United States' occupation of Iraq. He was also convicted of conspiracy to maltreat detainees, failing to protect detainees from abuse, cruelty, and maltreatment, as well as charges of assault, indecency, and dereliction of duty. A portion of the allegations involved Graner and others stacking nude Iraqi humans in a pyramid and forcing them to masturbate while he and other "soldiers" took photographs. Pictures of the sadistic Graner grinning near the lump of naked Iraqis were produced.

He was found guilty of all charges on January 14, 2005, and sentenced to ten years in prison, demotion to private, dishonorable discharge and forfeiture of pay and allowances. Charges of adultery and obstruction of justice were dropped before trial. Graner held the rank of Specialist in the company during his tour of duty in Iraq. While in Iraq, Specialist Lynndie England, also implicated in the prisoner scandal, became pregnant, allegedly by him ("Graner gets ten years for Abu Ghraib abuse" msnbc.com 1-16-2005; see also Charles Graner, Jr. in Wikipedia, which chronicles the events with numerous references). The trial occurred in Germany under US law. Graner disgraced two branches of the Armed Services, the Army and the Marines, as well the USA.

There are millions of unemployed people in Western Pennsylvania, and many more working men and women who are "underemployed." Many thousands of them would be tickled with a job as a prison guard: protected by a union, guaranteed work, and decently paid. But the State Correctional Facility in Greene passed by each and every other qualified person in order to hire this Charles A. Graner, Jr. as a corrections officer. It is as if a bride had the choice of all the great singing voices in world history to perform at her wedding, but shoved them all aside, leaping instead at the likes of a drunken Roseanne Barr or a Bob Dylan, un-showered. It is as if a child had his choice to be any creature in the sea for a day, from the fearsome killer whale to the brilliant dolphin to the languid manatee, from the stunning sergeant major to the beautiful French Angelfish, and that child thumbed its nose at all of them in favor of the putrid carp.

It should come as no surprise that SCI Greene is notorious for the racist abuse routinely dispensed by guards like Graner. In 1998, there was an uproar over abuse of prisoners, who complained that Graner and other turnkeys at the prison "routinely beat and humiliated prisoners, including through a sadistic game of Simon Says in which guards struck prisoners who failed to comply with barked instructions" (*New York Times*, 6 May 1998). In the beleaguered Greene SCI, several allegations involve Graner. The first occurred on July 29, 1998, Horatio Nimley, convicted of burglary, was eating mashed potatoes when his mouth started bleeding and he spat out a razor blade. According to a May 1999 federal lawsuit brought by Nimley against Graner, five other guards, and the prison nursing supervisor, Graner first planted the blade in his potatoes, ignored him, and finally brought him to the nurse, where they punched, kicked, and slammed Nimley on the floor. Nimley also alleges that when he screamed, "Stop, stop," Graner told him, "Shut up, nigger, before we kill you." Graner denies these allegations. A federal magistrate in Pittsburgh, however, ruled that the charges have "arguable merit in fact and law." However, when Nimley was released from prison in 2000, he disappeared, and the case was dismissed, leaving much of what happened still in question.

A second lawsuit involving Graner was brought by a prisoner who claimed that guards made him stand on one foot while handcuffed and tripped him. This allegation, however, was ruled to have been made too late, as the statute of limitations had expired. During his time at Greene, Graner was connected with several incidents of a violent nature. The *Washington Post* reported that "abuse allegations had become common at Greene . . . Guards beat prisoners, spit in their food, showered them with racial epithets and wrote 'KKK' in one beaten prisoner's blood. The allegations weren't without merit: In 1998, two dozen guards were fired, suspended, demoted, or reprimanded." One prison spokesman said none of the allegations involved Graner, which is very hard to believe. It is like the zookeeper telling us that the stink is not coming from the corner of the pen where there has lain a dead hippopotamus.

Nick Yarris, a former inmate who was recently released after DNA tests cleared him of rape and murder charges, spent twenty-two years on Death Row in SCI Greene. Yarris confirms the type of abuse Nimley alleged, recounting an incident in May 1998 when Yarris saw Graner and four other guards pull an inmate who purposefully flooded the toilet out of his cell and dragged him away. Yarris says Graner was holding a can of pepper spray and said, "We're going to go get some." Yarris says the inmate was severely bruised the next time he was seen.

Yarris also said Graner "bragged about taunting anti-death-penalty protesters who would gather outside the prison, used racial epithets, and once told a Muslim inmate he had rubbed pork all over his tray of food." In another interview, he said Graner was "responsible for moving prisoners within the facility and was 'violent, abusive, arrogant and mean-spirited.'"

Graner was fired from his job in July 2000, not for the abusive conduct but for walking off the job and not working a mandatory overtime shift on June 16. After filing a grievance, an arbitrator ruled after a July 2002 hearing that the firing was inappropriate, reducing it to a three-day suspension and ordering Graner reinstated with back pay (according to Wikipedia, World IQ, and other internet sources. Facts are readily verifiable).

This is a notorious example of a prison guard operating in the prison ghetto, but only because Graner became a world-renown criminal in the Abu Ghraib prison torture case. Graner's ability to walk through the raindrops at SCI Greene, or his dumb luck, probably led to a feeling of invincibility where he could expand his sadistic conduct overseas against the hated Iraqis. Sadly enough, the State Prison system in Pennsylvania proved to be a superb training ground for Graner's criminal antics at Abu Ghraib.

The jails are clearly unable to police themselves and their employees are generally able to escape detection and punishment for their abhorrent conduct because they are a part of "the system," along with the police, sheriffs, District Attorneys, and others on the side of the "law," and because their victims are the dregs of society who generate revulsion, not sympathy. The recipe is for subhuman, corrupt, and sick behavior, from which we easily turn our eyes.

A review of more prison cases over the past few years in Pennsylvania illustrates that the ghetto atmosphere in the jails is so prolific that it must be considered as a critical element in the criminal justice system. An "isolated case" here and there begins to add up to a norm. (Many of these cases are reported by the Prison Legal News at www. prisonlegalnews.com. If you are not soured on the prison scheme after reading the brief summary in this chapter, log on to the website. As painful as it is to read, it is difficult to stop reading, as one verified account of sadism is followed by another verified count of abuse. Although one should turn one's eyes from such debauchery, this is easier said than done. It is akin to watching a fat woman fall down a stairway. All cases referred to by the Prison Legal News have checked out as accurate, and cites have been provided where available.)

The overcrowding in our prisons leads to a host of problems. Budgets are squeezed with the accelerating costs of jails for both counties and states. Prisoners are bunked in hallways and gymnasiums. The overcrowding creates tension not only among the inmates, but also with the overburdened jail guards. Prisoners are routinely shuffled from one facility to another, often times several counties away. This opens up a number of opportunities for abuse, as if there were not enough already.

Prison guards have their own system of justice that occasionally is brought to the attention of the outside world. In Westmoreland County, just east of Pittsburgh, Judge Richard McCormick, Jr. inquired as to the source of prisoner Shawn Crider's black eyes and fresh bruises when he appeared for court on September 5, 2007. Crider's story that he was beaten by three guards while handcuffed in the jail's booking area, out of the view of camera surveillance, was trumped by the stories given by jail employees that Crider's injuries were due to an unfortunate "fall." No charges were pressed there but the Prison Board had to fire guard Scott Rogers, a ten-year veteran, earlier that year for making prisoners walk and bark like dogs, sing nursery rhymes, recite the alphabet, and kneel in uncomfortable positions with their foreheads pressed against the wall and their hands behind their heads. Rogers was actually charged with official oppression, as even the District Attorney could not overlook the concept that county prisoners were not meant to serve as the sadistic lunch meat of moronic jail turnkeys. Rogers pled guilty February 26, 2009 to three counts of official oppression. County officials rescinded the firing and allowed this lout, Rogers, to resign in order to protect themselves from a lawsuit if he was acquitted. The inmates Rogers abused were in a unit housing sex offenders and prisoners with mental health problems. The former Westmoreland County prison guard will serve nine months of probation for forcing inmates to submit to his demands of infantile sadism (Pittsburgh WDEQ News, February 2009, online).

More often, direct guard-on-prisoner violence and abuse is cleverly replaced by "prisoner justice," such as the case of Christopher S. Gilchrist, who was savagely beaten by fellow prisoner Mario Banegas while jail guard John Hampton and his cohort Charles Goodman watched and snickered. Gilchrist needed eight stitches to his pate and had a broken rib. Both Hampton and Goodman pleaded guilty to conspiracy to prisoner assault (Felony-2) and Unsworn Falsifications to Authority in November, 2007 and received five years' probation (Case nos. 2997, 2998-2007, Chester County, Pennsylvania). How many of such instances go unreported or are reported simply as routine prisoner-on-prisoner assaults? Obviously, guards Hampton and Goodman came out of the box lying in the Gilchrist investigation. Prisoner-on-prisoner assaults are rarely even dealt with by the disinterested courts other than having the offenders' parole denied for misconduct.

Hopefully, the United States of America can win Bill Clinton's "War on Drugs," which seeks to eradicate illegal drugs from society. In 1994, Clinton signed into law a massive federal crime bill that significantly expanded federal criminal jurisdiction, added new federal death penalties, a federal three-strikes rule, and increased punishments for hate crimes. Many states followed suit.

Or maybe we should set aside such delusions of grandeur and just concentrate on how to reduce drug trafficking in our own prisons. At present, we are quite feeble in that effort. According to the Pittsburgh Post-Gazette, a 2006 indictment involved four Allegheny County jail guards and two former guards, who were among eight people charged with smuggling drugs and other contraband into the 2,850-bed facility. The grand jury presentment set forth scenes of drug dealing and double dealing, secret codes and sexual favors, payoffs and paybacks among corrections officers conspiring with yardbirds. Allegheny County is not unique. A scandal in April 2004 at the Northumberland County Jail involved seven guards suspected of smuggling drugs into their own prison.

Jeremy Lensbouer smuggled heroin into the Somerset county jail in 2007. He pleaded guilty on February 21, 2007 to the Felony-2 charges (Cr. 554- 2006 Somerset County) and was sentenced to time served. Willie Freddy Franklin had already been convicted of felony drug charges in 2002 in his home county (Cr 5026-2002 Lancaster County), but that did not discourage the county jail from employing him as a turnkey. He exploited that opportunity adroitly in 2006 by smuggling into the jail significant quantities of heroin, cigarettes, and lighters.

Brian Sullivan will not get a chance at rehabilitation in prison. He died of a heroin overdose in April 2005 at George Hill Correctional Facility (GHCF). His was the second drug overdose in the facility and there were six other instances of unnatural deaths there between 2001 and 2006 (www.prisonlegalnews.org, Dec. 15, 2010). Deputy Superintendent John Reilly opined that some guards at the facility are using female co-workers as "mules" to smuggle contraband into the jail in their body cavities. Nonetheless, the GHFC was the first jail in Pennsylvania to receive accreditation by the American Correctional Association[6].

In Butler County, the new "state of the art" prison and its expertly trained guards were clueless when Martin J.

---

6 Id.

Mignogna was able to smuggle "a significant amount" of Suboxone, a drug connected with heroin addiction, and Xanax into the jail. This smuggling coup probably should not have bowled over the warden and his staff since Mignogna was already facing felony theft and drug charges. Mignogna chirped to county detectives on February 5, 2011 that he had concealed the drugs "in his body" (*Butler Eagle*, Feb. 8, 2011, p. 9). In the ghetto and on the street, users cannot be assured of the purity of the drugs they are sold by pushers and dealers, but at least they can assume with reasonable certainty that their illegal substances are not basted in a fecal marinade, which would have been the case with Mignogna's smuggled jail contraband unless he also possessed a vagina.

Ambrose Bierce defined prison as "a place of punishment and reward." Perhaps the most disgusting example of this could be found in the Dwight Correctional Center in Illinois. Stephen King could not have concocted a horror story this hideous. There, a former beauty pageant winner who became an inmate was gang raped by at least eight prison guards, plus others in the facility, twenty-nine times. Known as Jane Doe, the victim attempted to report the rapes but was shut down and threatened with an additional year of jail time. The story gets worse. Jane is afflicted with obstructive pulmonary lung disease and was forced to tote her oxygen tank with her to the bathroom where the rape squad would fornicate her. It gets worse again. She became pregnant from the rapes and, after her release, gave birth to a baby boy (www.prisonlegalnews.org/21225). She also gave birth to a Federal lawsuit against the prison[7]. If Dwight Correctional Center were a zoo, under these facts, the humane society and a number of other governmental agencies would have raced to close it down in order to

---

[7] *Doe v. Denning*, USDC (ND Ill) Case no. 1.2008-cv-01265.

protect defenseless animals from falling victim to curator criminal cruelty. But alas, DCC is just one of our prisons.

Joseph F. Henderson was a prison guard supervisor contracted to manage the GHCF prison. He was rewarded by a female prisoner who was forced to fellate him, with the threat of Henderson "interfering" with her parole hearing if she did not perform the requested sexual favor. Henderson was charged in December 2005 with two counts of sexual assault, bribery, and official oppression. This twerp pleaded guilty to a Misdemeanor-2 charge of official oppression and served a six to twenty-three-month term, but was also registered as a sexually violent offender (Case No. 8254-2005 Delaware County). Gregory A. Williams had his way with prisoners Melissa Torres and Helen McCandless-Weiss at the pristine Cambridge Springs Correctional Institution. Melissa and Helen were forced into oral sex with Williams, who also found time to manage the food service of the massive facility. Williams was found guilty of four counts of institutional sexual assault and one count of official oppression, and was acquitted of four pile-on charges. He received his due time of four months on October 8, 2008 (No. 621-2007 Crawford County).

The ghetto and the prison are very similar as to how internal justice is meted out. One of the less considered arguments for decriminalization of drugs is that, by forcing the players underground, there can be no peaceful enforcement of disputes over quantity or payments or over broken deals. This leads to violent dispute resolution. The underground guard/prisoner relationship is identically corrupt and violent.

The juices were flowing in the spring of 2008 for one Brandon Fraim. Fraim was finally charged with Institutional Sexual Assault in December 2008, after video cameras recorded him sneaking into the women prisoners' quarters and forcing himself upon at least four lady prisoners. This type of captive audience would not be available to Fraim in a real ghetto situation, but the prison program proved to be just the tonic he needed to edify his perversions. This Fraim, stupid to the end, reportedly clucked, "I just got caught up with flirting with young girls. They make it sound like there was sex, but it was just kissing." (PrisonLegalNews. org/21225 Display Article). It is the type of client that makes a defense attorney yearn for immediate retirement. Fraim would have to explain to Judge Charles H. Saylor (with the help of the video surveillance) how this innocent kissing that occurred behind prison bars could establish a felony charge. Judge Saylor accepted a no-contest plea to four counts of Institutional Sexual Assault, Felony-3 charges on July 27, 2008, in the Northumberland County Courthouse, which he could not have done unless there was something a little more risqué than a kiss on the cheek. The felon, Fraim, received nine to thirty-six months jail time for these untimely "kisses" (Case No. 233-2009 Northumberland County). Good buddy Gregg Cupp, a prison guard at the same facility, pleaded to Institutional Sexual Assault as well and went to jail for four and a half months (Case No. 124-2009 Northumberland County). It was reported that Deputy Warden John Conrad had shrugged off initial reports of the guards' misconduct as "silly talk" (PrisonLegalNews.org/21225). Perhaps a forewarning: John B. Conrad was guilty of a charge of disregarding a traffic signal in Northumberland County on February 9, 2001 (Case No. 111-2001, District Court 8-3-03).

Prison guards who are sexually frustrated have an open door inside prison walls. Ask any of the thirteen jail guards in Allegheny County who were arrested in a sex scandal in 2004 that involved trading contraband to prisoners in exchange for sexual favors. Ask Bedford County Prison Guard William Robert Lewis, Jr., who raped a prisoner in a bathroom in January 2006. He pleaded guilty to the felony count on July 21, 2007 (Cr 112-2006 Bedford County). He is out of jail now, having served forty-five days. Ask the victims of seven guards and a kitchen worker at the Monroe County Correctional Facility where illegal sexual contact with them was discovered, leading to the arrests of Dana Simpson and Roodney Ulysse (no-contest pleas) and Yvonne Lockard and Karen Stone (guilty pleas). At least in the Monroe County battery of criminal charges the prisoners wound up with cell phones in exchange for the forced sex. Many prisoners get nothing for their services. Four other guards and workers were charged with smuggling drugs into the Monroe County Prison for money and sex.

Police utilize prisons to get in on the act as well, such as Norberto Cappas, who required two women to perform a Vegas style sex show for him in the privacy of their detention cell. The women were forced into lesbian sexual acts that included exposing their boobs. One of them has sued the city. During the investigation it was determined that the women had no business being detained in the first place and that Cappas (surprise) had lied during the investigation. He was fired, but the humiliation and damage was irreversible (www.prisonlegalnews.org, 2007).

The prison scheme provides a superb opportunity for bribery and corruption even if the guards involved are asexual. The corruption at the Lackawanna County Jail has been stupid, petty, and insipid. The Warden, Thomas P. Gilhooley, his Deputy, Robert A. Hilborn, a Sergeant, Anthony Veno, and a Lieutenant, Leonard Bogdanski, were charged with theft of services and violating state ethics laws. What they did was use prison inmates to decorate their homes for Christmas, gut and rebuild a room in their house, repair wrecked vehicles, restore classic cars, and detail their private cars with prison supplies. Prisoners received extra furlough time, food, favors, and cash payments as bribes[8]. All were charged and convicted of ungraded felonies under

---

8 Id.

"Restricted Activities" (65 P.S. 403) in criminal court (Cases No. 1259, 1531, 1543, and 1650 of 2004 Lackawanna County).

We could go on and on. A December 2007 Bureau of Justice Statistics report estimated that 38,600 state and federal prisoners had self-reported sexual abuse or misconduct by prison employees. This number represents just the tip of the iceberg. For every prisoner who would risk retaliation with a false charge of that nature, there are many more who fail to report legitimate incidents for fear of retribution, embarrassment, and a sullen acknowledgement that their cries would most likely fall on deaf ears. But to put that number in perspective—38,600 self-reported sexual abuse or misconduct victims in U.S. prisons—consider that it is greater than the entire number of prisoners in the country of Iraq, which has a population of about thirty million! It is more than all the prisoners in the nations of Greece, Portugal, Austria, and Switzerland combined. If we lined up all the prisoners in the United States who have reported to have been sexually abused, and lined up all the prisoners in the entire continent of Australia, the U.S.A.'s line would be longer.*

The message of corruption, bribery, smuggling, rape, etc. is perhaps not the best message to be sending to persons incarcerated for criminal acts who must eventually be released back into society. The only difference, it seems, between the prisoner and the keeper is who gets caught committing crimes. What mindset do the prisoners learn from this program? These glaring defects in corrections are apparently lost upon the politicians legislating mandatory prison terms for various crimes. However, should not the ghetto atmosphere of the prison be a factor the legislatures must consider when another mandatory sentence sounds good to them?

---

* (*World Prison Population List*, 8th edition, King's College London 2008)

# CHAPTER 2

# Faith Hopski And
# A Win For The Dim

There is no fool like a young fool. Faith Hopski, a twenty-one-year-old nursing student, got into the Margaritas and Coors Light on June 4, 2005. Faith was a student with a part-time job at a Pizza joint in Mercer, which was run by a retired State Trooper. She was a jolly young lady who appeared to the close observer as a cross between Sally Struthers and Elton John—a bit too heavy for her shorts and a gap between her front teeth. But on that June 4th Faith had a night out that she will never forget.

Driving through some God-forsaken back roads in Mercer County, Pennsylvania for reasons no one could determine, her car took an erratic maneuver and went off the right side of the road. The vehicle continued to slip to the right and became hung up on a strand of metal. It was bottomed out. Faith's mobility at this point in time was almost precisely equivalent to that of a pushed-over cow. She eventually closed down all efforts to move the vehicle. Faith was very intoxicated and could not solve the mystery of dialing 9-1-1 or otherwise calling for help on her cell phone. She did what any dim but drunk person would do; she crawled into the back seat to sleep it off.

Her first issue was that the strand of metal she was stuck on happened to be the property of the Bessemer and Lake Erie Railroad. She was stuck square in the middle of a railroad track—not a recommended location in which to sleep off a drunken stupor. Fortunately, the first passerby saw the obvious train wreck waiting to happen and stopped to offer assistance. Faith was so intoxicated that she could not be aroused. The car was still running and the wheels still spinning from her futile efforts. The good Samaritan, along with another helper, pulled her out of the back seat and moved her into a safer position, which could have been in a bear cave at that point. But Faith was positioned along the road, fifty feet away from the railroad tracks and her car. She was out of harm's way for the time being.

The only thing that could possibly make matters worse now was about to happen. The police arrived. While police seldom interrupt the scenes of burglaries, robberies, or assaults, they usually can find a DUI, and here the police managed to find their way to this remote area of the County to confront Ms. Hopski. She was still oblivious to the situation. The cop told her to "sit tight" while he investigated. He found out nothing of value other than what was already obvious, to wit: Faith's vehicle was stuck on railroad tracks. She appeared to be intoxicated. There was no sign of any other driver, although Faith was found in the back seat. The railway was notified and the vehicle was moved into safety. The plates were traced and came back to Faith as the owner of the vehicle.

Now what to do with Faith? It was clear from the testimony that no one had any idea how long the vehicle had been stuck on the railroad tracks. With regard to an arrest, the police were in a quandary. The chemical test to deter-

---

*Commonwealth v. HLW* (No. 920-2005 Mercer County)

Parking for Yardbirds Only. All others will be towed at owners' expense.

mine alcohol concentration must be taken within two hours of the defendant's operation of the vehicle. Could this be a situation where someone is simply helped out of a bad spot with no alacrity, but a valuable lesson learned?

No. Not in this era. It was apparently critical for the Commonwealth that a DUI arrest occur in Mercer County, Pennsylvania that night. The officer was on a mission. But instead of giving Faith her Miranda warnings and requesting permission to interview her, he plowed forward and questioned her on what happened. She admitted being the driver and she admitted drinking alcoholic beverages. (This is a full confession in police custody.) She refused, however, to submit to a blood alcohol test to determine the level of intoxication she was enjoying. In this situation, the law presumed that she was at the highest statutory rate, a reasonable presumption under this scenario. But unbeknownst to Faith, this critical decision placed her into a category of DUI where a mandatory term of imprisonment (ninety days to five years) would be imposed if she were convicted of driving under the influence of alcohol.

Pennsylvania's wild and crazy DUI law has a number of weird quirks. It was drafted by the Legislature at the eleventh hour in 2004 when Federal monies for highway programs were to be linked with a nationwide crusade against drunk driving. States were required to lower their threshold for BAC levels to .08, among other things. The chemical test sample must be obtained within two hours of when the Defendant last operated the vehicle. This has led to many high speed police chases—chases from the scene of a DUI arrest to a local hospital for a blood draw, cops bowling over ER personnel to get to the phlebotomist's table, and other such asinine scenes. Pennsylvania's DUI law has kept defense attorneys busy ever since its historic enactment.

Here is one example of the incongruous aspects of the law applied to Ms. Hopski. For second-time offenders, a drunk driver in the highest level of alcohol testing (above .16 percent) faces a Misdemeanor-1 charge, which is the equivalent of aggravated assault without a deadly weapon. Worse, it requires an eighteen-month suspension of operating privileges, and a MANDATORY jail sentence of ninety days plus a probationary period of five years!

On the contrary, if the drinking driver's blood test comes in between .10 and .16 percent, one falls in the level of an ungraded misdemeanor, equivalent to a Misdemeanor-3 disorderly conduct charge. This offender is facing only thirty days in jail with a six-month probation period. The operator's license is suspended for one year. Thus a driver with a .159 Blood alcohol concentration faces penalties substantially less than that of a driver with a .161, despite the well-proven scientific fact that blood alcohol tests are only accurate, at best, to a 10 percent margin of error.

But it gets better. An individual with an "accident enhancement" DUI is placed in the intermediate level, an ungraded misdemeanor, versus the high BAC offender who may have driven safely. We have had many cases like this.

Under Pennsylvania's DUI law, as it now reads, one is better off crashing his vehicle into a school bus with a BAC of .159 than he is driving perfectly fine into his garage with a BAC of .161. And not just a little better off, as we have just seen. Since 2004, this incredible scenario is replayed on a daily basis in Pennsylvania.

■

In defending Faith, I challenged the government's ability to prove that she was the driver of the vehicle. Although she owned the vehicle, it is not beyond the realm of possibility that someone else drove her home from the party and when the driver disabled the vehicle, he or she panicked and left the scene, knowing (or not knowing) that Faith decided to pass out in the back seat. It was not our burden to disprove that she was driving; it was the government's burden to prove that she was. This was an essential element of the offense of DUI that would have to be proven beyond a reasonable doubt. The only evidence that Faith was driving came from her own drunken mouth after she was clearly a suspect in the case. She should have been Mirandized and warned that under the Fifth Amendment to the United States Constitution she had an absolute right *not* to speak to the police and give them evidence to aid in their prosecution of her.

My motion to suppress her statements was denied. The court ruled that the Miranda warnings were not necessary until Faith was in police custody, i.e., until she was *not* free to leave the scene. Next was the trial. In this situation, it is pointless to have a jury trial since the Judge would instruct the jury that her statement admitting driving would be enough to satisfy the element of "driving" and the intoxication could be established by the policeman's testimony and the circumstantial evidence of the bad driving and stuporous condition after the vehicle was disabled. We had a bench trial (before the judge only) just to preserve the issue for appeal that Faith should have been Mirandized.

Having failed in my attempt to suppress her statement that provided the Commonwealth with one of the two elements of the offense, I now turned to the strategy of minimizing her damages at sentencing. The sentencing stage occurs prior to the appeal. I argued that she should not be penalized for being in the highest level of alcohol since (1) there was no blood alcohol test and (2) if there was a blood alcohol test, there was no way to establish that the blood test was done within two hours of the time of the last driving. Therefore, even though she refused the BAC test, she should not be penalized for this since a test would have been worthless as untimely. The court had to agree with this astoundingly profound logic, and instead of facing the Misdemeanor-1 charge, it was agreed that, at worst, Faith would be guilty under the "accident enhancement" provision of the law, the ungraded misdemeanor.

Faith was evaluated for alcohol treatment and was prescribed some help, of which she availed herself. The Sentencing Judge imposed the mandatory term of incarceration of thirty days in the county jail, but permitted that term to be served on House Arrest with Electronic Monitoring. This would be followed by five months' probation.

We appealed the decision on the Miranda violation to the Superior Court of Pennsylvania. The Superior Court upheld the trial court's decision that Faith's Right against Self Incrimination was not violated. I felt this decision was absolutely wrong. Ms. Hopski was clearly in police custody and the subject of a criminal investigation when she was told to "sit tight" by the officer. But the ruling of the Court is what counted in this case, not my position on the Constitution.

■

What was even more unusual about this appeal and this case was that the Superior Court, *sua sponte* (on its own initiative), asked both me and the District Attorney to submit briefs on the issue of whether or not the Sentencing Court had the authority to grant house arrest or whether the mandatory thirty days was to be served behind prison bars.

There are several obvious points from this case and some not so obvious. For our purposes here in this chapter, the significance is not particularly what happened with the criminal case, as bizarre as it may have been. Nor is it the court's erosion of an individual's right against self-incrimination for the purpose of sustaining a criminal conviction. This, sadly, occurs on a daily basis as well. The point of this chapter is the issue of the mandatory sentencing provisions of the DUI law. It is their contribution to the overcrowding of the prisons around the country, and in this particular case, the Commonwealth of Pennsylvania.

In the odd second phase to our appeal, the Superior Court decided to make an issue over whether or not the mandatory imprisonment language of the DUI sentencing statute trumped the statue setting forth eligibility requirements for Intermediate Punishment (house arrest). House arrest allows an individual to serve a term of imprisonment without ever setting foot in a jail, though the person is a convicted criminal and is in fact imprisoned in his or her own home. Typically, the house arrestee is permitted to leave the house only for purposes of work, school, counseling, medical or legal appointments, or other pre-approved emergency situations. The subject is hooked up to a monitor that registers a signal to the house arrest supervisors if he or she leaves his designated pen or removes the collar. It is the same concept used to contain dogs in a confined area, the difference being that a dog is merely shocked when he crosses the line, whereas a house arrestee is taken into prison for a technical house arrest violation

In addition, most arrestees are required to randomly submit to an alcohol monitoring test, random urine tests, and other visits from Intermediate Punishment bureaucrats. In this sense the animal has more freedom since no one from the government monitors its food and beverage intake, aside from quantity perhaps. No firearms or alcohol are permitted in these premises, to complete the dulcification of the subject. The cost can be upwards of $20 per day.

As restrictive, burdensome, and humiliating as house arrest is, most defendants would prefer this to a prison setting, even if work release is permitted. The comforts of home are still available to some extent. More importantly, the company is much better even if the arrestee lives with in-laws. One of the major complaints from those serving first-time jail sentences in the county prison is the forced association with criminals, meatheads, and screwballs, and we are not just referring to the guards. First-time offenders or repeat DUI offenders do not place themselves in any of these ribald categories. The forced association and submission to the rules and whims of the jail guard turn-key are unbearable to the yardbird of average or above-average intelligence. The infantile game of "good cop," "bad cop" played between the turn-keys and the prisoners grates on this caliber of yardbird. The prison setting for the average American is mental torture to all except the most brutal dullards.

The prisons could not possibly accommodate all the people we now convict without house arrest programs. In Faith Hopski's case, the District Attorney's office was obviously unconcerned with this demographic and logistical issue when it took the position on appeal that the mandatory imprisonment provisions of the DUI statute trumped the house arrest statute, the opposite position that we argued. Some of the arguments in the District Attorney's brief to support their position were nothing more than base

21

recitation of very general rules of law. ("The term 'imprisonment' is clear and unambiguous and should be given
effect in accordance with its plain and common meaning.")
Their argument did have some specious merit in that the
Intermediate Punishment statue enacted in 2004, which
made second-time offenders for DUI eligible for house
arrest, was enacted before the DUI law in 2004, which
made a penalty for DUI offenders "mandatory imprisonment." In effect, the District Attorney argued that since the
DUI mandatory sentence was enacted after the Intermediate Punishment eligibility section, the mandatory imprisonment provision of the DUI law, which does not make
provision for house arrest, supersedes the house arrest
eligibility section. "Clearly, the Legislative intent was to
require a mandatory minimum amount of imprisonment,
not intermediate punishment" (Appellee's Brief p. 5). Sad
to say, that probably was the Legislative intent.

We had an uphill battle on this argument as well. We
argued that the eligibility requirements for Intermediate Punishment in the IPP statute included eligibility
requirements for DUI offenders. Since eligibility for DUI
offenders is specifically addressed in the IPP statute, those
requirements would trump the mandatory jail provisions
of the DUI statute. Under the general sentencing laws of
Pennsylvania (42 Pa. C.S.A. 9721), the court must impose
a mandatory jail sentence "unless specifically authorized
by (the IPP statute)." The main requirement that an individual must satisfy for a subsequent DUI offender to qualify
for IPP under house arrest is that he or she must be evaluated for Drug and/or Alcohol dependency.

Fortunately for Ms. Hopski, and thousands of others, the
Superior Court sided with us on the issue of house arrest eligibility. The court held that her sentence of house arrest was
proper, as it "imposed IPP for her second DUI offense so
long as the program is a qualified court IPP program and she

is a qualified 'eligible offender,'" Since she had participated in and completed a Drug and Alcohol assessment, Ms. Hopski was, in fact, an eligible offender. Thus the Court held that the IPP statute defining eligibility trumped the DUI mandatory jail sentence language, a close call. The Superior Court of Pennsylvania, in this singular opinion, kept thousands of individuals convicted of DUI out of their county prisons by making them eligible for house arrest (*Commonwealth v. HW*, 827 WDA 2006, Pa Super. Ct.).

In 2010, the Pennsylvania State Police set a record for the ninth straight year in making Driving Under the Influence arrests. The figure for 2010 was 17,695. This number does not include arrests for DUI by all municipal police departments. The record-breaking figures prove one of two things: 1. Pennsylvanians are oblivious to the new DUI law and its more penal effects. The new law does not act as a deterrent and is a failure. 2. Pennsylvania has stepped up DUI deployments to make more arrests for DUI because the money is good for the state. Picking off the low-hanging DUI fruit is easier and more lucrative than investigating and arresting real criminals. Either one of the two, or both, are true. The government cannot have it both ways.

Christine M. Rokoski of Butler County would probably argue that both of the above are true. She had called the State Police to assist with a child custody issue and was not able to speak to a Trooper. Rather than be abused by her ex-paramour, she took her eleven-year-old son from the potentially violent situation at the home and went directly to the police barracks. She parked her SUV at the station and went in to talk to a Trooper face to face. The officer wanted nothing of the domestic dispute but his interest was perked when he smelled beer on Rokoski's breath. When she tested at .137 percent BAC, they arrested her for DUI and child endangerment ("Woman Charged With DUI After Driving to Police Station," *Butler Eagle*, Apr. 22, 2011, p. 8).

In the Faith Hopski case, the District Attorney's natural instinct to oppose anything that did not restrict the freedom of an offender nearly created a statewide jail burst. Prosecutors are advocates for the government and are elected to be tough on crime in their localities. If defense attorneys take a position, the prosecutor must take the opposite position, no matter how dunderheaded it may be. And some prosecutors develop a fetishistic desire to incarcerate everyone in their path. This attitude is not likely to change, nor should it, *so long as the playing field is level.*

On the contrary, this grave flaw in our system would melt away if the mandatory jail sentences set by the legislature were overturned or repealed. The District Attorneys feel compelled to argue for and uphold the Legislative sentence mandates, even though, as will be discussed later, these sentence mandates from the legislature form the basis of a breach of the separation of powers—one of the fundamental safeguards of our constitution.

# CHAPTER 3

# Mercer County, Pennsylvania

Mercer County is a political subdivision of the Commonwealth of Pennsylvania, located between Pittsburgh and Erie. It is classic "rust-belt" territory. Sharon, Farrell, Greenville, West Middlesex, and other small towns have been reduced to mere shells of what they once were. When the country goes into a recession, this is the first area to be hit. When recovery begins, it is the last area to move out of the malaise. The Director of the Regional Planning Committee for the County has dubbed this phenomenon FILO, "First In Last Out." The most recent recession in 2008-2009 has beaten down the region so thoroughly it is left with little hope of ever regaining relative economic prosperity.

But that has not stopped the prison business from prospering.

We will take a look at Mercer County because it may well be a window as to what is occurring in many counties and states across the northeast and perhaps even elsewhere across the nation. Looking at the statistics for prison populations statewide and nationwide, Mercer County is obviously not an isolated situation.

In its period of growth, Mercer County's population expanded rapidly. The following chart shows population growth in the county. Population leveled in the 1970s and in the 1980s the population peaked. In the most recent censuses Mercer County, Pennsylvania actually show a decline in population. These statistics understate the emigration from the area because the remaining inhabitants include the severely aged (who have expanded rapidly in number) versus the younger, productive members of society who have bolted from the area to find decent jobs. The population continues towards decrepitation.

Next we compare the population of the county *in toto* to the prison population. Here we bear witness to a microcosm of YardBird USA.

The first separate prison structure in Mercer County was a simple stone jail holding about ten prisoners. It was built in 1810 at a cost of $3,000. This structure was good enough until 1868.

**The Old Stone Jail on Venango Street, Mercer County's first jail**

In 1869 a new jail was built on South Diamond Street holding about twenty prisoners. This jail cost about $67,000, which included a tunnel to transport prisoners under South Diamond Street to the Mercer County Courthouse. During the time period from 1810 to 1870, the population of Mercer County had rapidly increased from 8,227 to 49,977, so the need for a larger prison was quite obvious (Mercer County, Pennsylvania Pictorial History 1800-2000, Mercer County Historical Society, 2001, pp. 95, 98-99).

**Second Mercer County Jail, South Diamond St., Mercer**

The above sensibly located and stately jail was not outgrown until the 1970s, nearly a century anon. Then a new prison was built just a few buildings away in 1976. Capacity at that time was twenty-four prisoners plus twelve work release confines (see below).

All hell was breaking loose in the legislature and the courts, and this prison was too small before the doors had even opened up. The facility expanded wildly in 1990, and could now accommodate 114 prisoners, an exponential increase over all prior prisons in just fourteen short years (MCPH, p. 469). All of these prisons were located within a block from the County Courthouse so prisoners could easily be shuffled from their cells to the courthouse for their hearings.

**Third Mercer County Jail, South Diamond St., Mercer, expanded in 1990 from 36 to 114 capacity**

However, this was not enough. Just fourteen years later, while the anile population of the county as a whole was shrinking, businesses closing, and young people moving away from the area to find employment, the Mercer County Commissioners went on an incredible foray. In 2006, a brand new County Prison was constructed about four miles away from the courthouse. This fantastic structure holds over two hundred fifty yard birds, cost the taxpayers untold million dollars and is already too small! In 2010-2011 the county had forced expenditures on the septic system, which had quickly erupted, having outgrown its expected capacity almost immediately.

**New Mercer County Prison—West Side**

**New Mercer County Prison—East Side**

The new Mercer County Prison and its burdensome expenses do not stop with construction and expansion of the sewage bed. Instead of having prisoners walked across the street for their court dates, we have now hired several deputy sheriffs with more vehicles to transport them to and from their cells to the county courthouse four miles away. Obviously, the taxpayers are putting out for this totally worthless activity, creating a further drag on an already sickly economy.

County real estate taxes increased from 18.75 mils to 22.75 mils from 2004 to 2008, in part to fund the new prison. One mil is equivalent to $1/1000, or .001 percent. On a property assessed at $100,000 the county taxes alone would have increased from $1,875 per year to $2,275 per year, a jump of 21.3 percent. Added to this are the school taxes and the municipal taxes. The total tax burden now averages about 100 mils in the county of Mercer. Thus we have now reached a point where in ten years a property owner will have paid the entire assessed value of his or her property back to government in real estate taxes.

The following is another perspective on our demented prison scheme: If one were to pile up all of the prisoners who could totally fill the Mercer County jail in 1989 and then pile up beside them all of the Mercer County prisoners in 2011 who are on "suicide watch," this second pile would be 1 ½ times higher than the first pile. It has been reported that 56 prisoners in the Mercer County Jail are on suicide watch as of this writing. FN: (The Herald, "Board Eyes Jail Med Care Report," by Lauren Mylo, July 27, 2011), whereas the entire jail population in 1989 was just 36!

At the present rate Mercer County will build another prison in 2015. The prison population will double again by 2020 and the general population will decline in that time period to 109,000. By applying complicated formulas I have retained from my college class in statistics, it is clear that the general population in Mercer County will decline to approximately 46,000 by the year 2110. By 2114, a short century away, the prison population in Mercer County will exceed 53,000, so based upon current trends there will be more people incarcerated than on the streets and in the hospitals in early 2111, just in time for Super Bowl 145. Unless I err, these calculations would be statistically correct.

■

My suspicion that Mercer County is not alone in this sick, demographical twist is confirmed by the conduct of neighboring counties throughout the state and across the nation. Butler County just constructed a monstrous prison to confine their swelling prison population. It is a 512 bed structure taking up a city block with an initial price tag of $30 million. But the price went up as it was being built and cost overruns and delays have caused lawsuits between the contractor and the county (www.PrisonLegalNews.org, December 15, 2010).

**Butler County Prison. Capacity 512. Cost $30 million+**

**The Spectacular Lawrence County Prison**

This spiffy new structure is about the tallest building in the city and has required the hiring of an additional sixty-five deputy sheriffs and correction officers. The City of Butler's population has fallen below 14,000 so now nearly one in twenty-seven Butler inhabitants will reside in this effulgent fortress.

Lawrence County was actually the first in our area to expand, building a magnificent brick prison across from the County Courthouse for an unknown sum, which holds three hundred prisoners. This prison has been over capacity almost from "Day 1" and in 2005, just shortly after its grand opening, one inmate died of a drug overdose. Another attempted suicide by jumping headfirst from a twelve-foot-high walkway. A third suffered a severe brain injury in a beating by another prisoner, and the work-release program had to be suspended after inmates were accused of smuggling drugs into the jail.*

___

* (December 21, 2005 PA: County Jails Encounter Major Problems, PA county jails no escape from big-prison problems, MARK SCOLFORO, Associated Press, Posted Tue, Dec. 20, 2005; www.centredaily.com/mld/centredaily/news/local/13450549.htm)

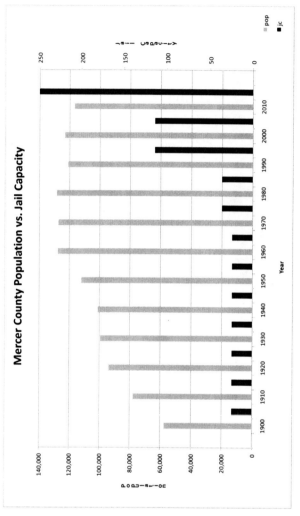

Mercer County Population vs. Jail Capacity

Mary C. Smeltzer

| Mercer County, Pennsylvania | | |
|---|---|---|
| Year | Population | Jail Capacity |
| 1900 | 57,387 | 24 |
| 1910 | 77,699 | 24 |
| 1920 | 93,788 | 24 |
| 1930 | 99,246 | 24 |
| 1940 | 101,039 | 24 |
| 1950 | 111,954 | 24 |
| 1960 | 127,519 | 24 |
| 1970 | 127,175 | 36 |
| 1980 | 128,299 | 36 |
| 1990 | 121,003 | 114 |
| 2000 | 123,007 | 114 |
| 2010 | 116,638 | 250 |

All around the state of Pennsylvania prison capacities are being expanded to accommodate more of our people and new prisons are being constructed at the expense of working people. Bear in mind that prisons are not cheap buildings. These are unique structures with the required security and protection of officers and visitors. Initial construction costs are generally $65,000 to $100,000 per bed.

**Yardbird USA**

# CHAPTER 4

# Jessica Gilson and
# the Snowball Effect

On December 13, 2007, just a few months after she turned eighteen years old, a troubled young lady named Jessica Gilson committed her first retail theft in Butler County Pennsylvania. Coming from a broken family, this high school dropout with no skills for work, a diagnosis of bipolar personality disorder, and a substance abuse problem, had a future that looked as bleak as a rainy winter night in Butler, Pennsylvania.

Her petty theft offense was committed with the help of others and the actual charge was a conspiracy. Due to the amount of merchandise stolen (over $150) the offense was graded a First Degree Misdemeanor with an offense gravity score of "2," which is on a level with Insults to Flag, Scattering Rubbish, and sexual intercourse with an animal.

She was kept in jail for fifteen days and then released on probation for six months. Her substance abuse and mental health issues led her to wander into the very same store once again, and she faced defiant trespass and retail theft

---

*Com. v. MG-Butler County* CR 1154-2008

charges on March 10, 2008. Her probation was revoked and directly into the county calaboose she went.

It seemed as though it would be a typical course of events. Young girl with substance abuse problems steals to feed her habit, is caught, placed in jail, released, re-offends, jailed at a state prison, takes rehabilitation courses, and is released again into the wild. This rotation is repeated time and time again all across the country. The prisons are full of petty thieves, some stealing for drug money, others stealing to eat, and many single mothers just stealing the basic survival staples for their children at Big Lots and Family Dollar stores. I have represented mothers with absolutely no money who were stealing coats and socks for their children in the winter so they would not freeze. Most of the time the thief is identified, the merchandise is returned, and it is extremely rare that anyone is injured.

Should these pitiable thieves be filling up our prisons or should they be given to wear orange badges stating "I am a convicted shoplifter?" Then, if they are discovered in a retail establishment without their badge conspicuously displayed, they can be incarcerated. This solution is offered only half in jest—certainly there are many better punishment options that do not involve imprisonment. The recidivist stats on retail theft offenders prove that jail is not a deterrent anyway[9].

Jessica Gilson is a superb example of why such a person should not be imprisoned for petty retail thefts. On April 23, 2008, just a few short weeks after she had the prison doors slammed behind her for stealing a Diet Snapple, flames and smoke poured from the old Butler County Prison.

---

9 *Incarcerated Mothers The Chicago Project on Female Prisoners and Their Children Initial Report*, June 2002 The University of Chicago.

Jessica and some of her female friends set a fire in the woman's unit. One of the girls had smuggled in tobacco from a court hearing earlier that day. (Her attempt to smuggle in stamps of heroin with a feminine maxi pad failed when she was unable to use the courthouse bathroom, but she did get the pads and took out the cotton center.) Another girl inserted lead pencils into the electrical outlet, which caused the outlet to spark. The cotton from the pad was easily ignited and then the girls enjoyed a smoke in the bathroom.

After their cigarette break, the girls developed a plan to set the jail on fire. The main goal was a modest one: to burn the screen out of the window and kick it open, then escape into the evening rush hour where they could see their boyfriends. They re-utilized the lead pencils to generate sparks. This time the sparks caught toilet paper on fire, followed by a pile of papers (a prisoner's GED work) resting on a bed.

These were not great criminal minds at work. The plan created much smoke but little fire, although a mattress did smolder wildly. A first alarm sounded, then a louder one. The alarms and the smoke alerted sleepy jail turnkeys, who, by instinct, called the police and fire departments from their customary seated positions. The girls were herded into the visiting area rather than outside, so no one could escape the confines of the Butler County Prison to smooch with their boyfriends on the street.

Photographs of the burnt mattress were taken by the Corporal. The girls were isolated and interviewed, all giving different versions of the great conspiracy. Jessica was clearly a lamb following more powerful and mature ewes. Under her bunk was the pencil with no lead, rolled- up paper, and maxi-cotton. She was in the game, but clearly a dim-witted pawn.

After the investigation was complete, Jessica was charged with a Felony One Count of Arson, a Felony One

Count of Causing or Risking a Catastrophe, and twenty-four counts of Recklessly Endangering Another Person, representing the danger she exposed the other yardbirds and responding personnel to by her activities that evening. The Arson charge was an offense gravity score of nine, on the same level as an armed robbery or a house burglary with an owner present.

Taking a look at the potential penalties, each Felony-1generated twenty years exposure to state prison and each Misdemeanor-2 REAP charge carried a two-year maximum, being another forty-eight years if run consecutively. The total exposure for this nineteen-year-old child was now eighty-eight years. A $25,000 bail was set. The state was taking this case very seriously, although not a soul was injured or even sought medical treatment as a result of the ordeal, and even the jail turnkeys were laughing about it by the time of the Preliminary Hearing.

My defense at trial was not that the fire was a figment of the imagination of the turnkeys or that the alarms were false. Clearly the fire was set. My defense was that the witnesses implicating Jessica as a major player in the catastrophe were so bad that a jury might discount their testimony entirely. Each co-conspirator scheduled to testify against Jessica had earned a significant criminal record. The principal architect of the conspiracy had compiled a record so profound that it took a separate file folder for me to carry the paperwork in. And many of the charges she stood convicted of involved crimes of *"crimen falsi"* or dishonesty (theft, forgery, etc.), which could be used as direct impeachment against her. The government's case against Jessica was not, perhaps, as strong as they had hoped.

Fortunately, due to this fancy legal work by her defense team and the employment of common sense by the prosecution, Jessica was offered a plea to one consolidated count of Reckless Endangerment, and a count of Conspiracy to

Commit Arson, with a recommended sentence of eleven to twenty-three months, followed by thirty-six months probation. If necessary, she agreed to testify against the mastermind of the foiled Butler County Jail Arson bid. Essentially this was to be one- to five-year term to be served in the county with the possibility of work release.

Jessica completed the Jail's Drug and Alcohol rehabilitation class, attended the jail's church and AA meetings, was "pod" cleaner for seven months, and she achieved her GED (High School Graduate Equivalent Degree). This was no small feat for a girl of very limited intelligence and the attention span of a fish. She served 261 days in jail as of the date of her sentence, which was January 15, 2009. She has a tough road ahead of her when she is released from jail and the eyes of the state will be following her movements for many years to come.

This case illustrates how the system used the easy way out and jailed this imbecilic young lady for petty offenses. While on parole, she was nothing more than a prisoner waiting for a bed—waiting for the day she violated her probation by committing another offense. Her problems—psychological, addictive and financial—were never addressed.

More than that, this case illustrates how imprisonment frequently compounds itself, how a person, once a prisoner, frequently re-offends out of stupidity and ends up behind bars again, only to create bigger and more profound problems that lead to longer incarcerations. It shows how an individual, once imprisoned, becomes a vehicle greasing a system that has run out of control. Is the prisoner or society served justice in a case like this one?

# CHAPTER 5

# The Taxpayers' Taj Mahal:
# Allegheny County

If you cross the ancient Smithfield Street Bridge from Station Square and enter the downtown area of Pittsburgh, Pennsylvania on a late summer afternoon, you will notice how the sun illuminates the city skyline and highlights the diverse and unique architectural features of some of this nation's great buildings. The view to the right, down the Monongahela River, is a striking one, especially when your eyes become drawn to a mammoth structure that now dominates the skyline around the Second Street area. It is a five-part building designed by L. Robert Kimball and Associates woven together masterfully. It cost more to construct than Donald Trump's crown jewel property in Atlantic City, the Trump Taj Mahal.

I have never had the occasion to visit this magnificent structure, and its website is somewhat vague as to exactly what amenities are provided on a consistent basis. The tour guides in Pittsburgh mention basketball courts, fitness centers, theatres, a library, cable TV, AC, good food and beverage, etc. No swimming pool is visible from the outside. The rooms are apparently nothing to write home about, but with all the activities available, one wouldn't expect to spend a lot of time in there, unless one was tuckered out from playing basketball and had fetched a really good book from the library.

This modern building replaced a much more modest structure that had long since been outgrown. The previous old structure was a practical and historically renowned masterpiece designed by Henry Hobson Richardson, located directly adjacent to the Allegheny County Courthouse. It was adequate for over a century, having been built in 1884-1886 and not being closed until 1995. It had a maximum capacity of 580, but this was stretching it by all accounts. However, in less than one decade, even the monstrous new building could not hold the numbers being tossed its way. The capacity of over 2,300 occupants was already obsolete.

Yes, the building we honor is the "new" Allegheny County Jail (built in 1995). The court had set a jail population cap of 580 inmates in the old jail, and stipulated that the county would be fined $25,000 for every month in which the cap was exceeded. On the other hand, however, the court also imposed a fine of $5,000 for "every prisoner released to meet the court-ordered population cap . . ." Illustrating how wildly the prison population was exploding, the amount of this latter fine was reduced in 1989 from $5,000 to $100. But the principle is the same: the jail cap cannot be exceeded on one hand, and the county is penalized when it releases inmates in order to comply with the cap on the other. It is a dichotomy that should not be lost upon the courts and the legislature, but it is. Between November 16, 1983, and December 30, 1990, 11,319 inmates in Allegheny County had to be released under these circumstances. "Relief for this situation is fortunately on the horizon," crowed the warden. "Allegheny County will break ground in the fall of 1991 for a new jail to be occupied by 1993" (sic), which was wishful thinking as the jail failed to open until 1995 (Charles Kozakiewicz, Warden, Allegheny County Jail, Pittsburgh, Pennsylvania).

This hulking landmark is truly a reflection of our society today. It reflects the enormous cost we bear of building and maintaining a prison used to incarcerate our fellow citizens. It reflects the corpulent prison population itself—bursting at its rotted seams—filled beyond capacity almost before it is opened. It reflects the power and weight of government in our lives. A major structure in the great City of Pittsburgh suddenly emerges in the skyline in 1995, a structure built by and for the government, maintained and operated by the government, full of inmates incarcerated by the government. It truly is reflective of a system totally overwhelmed by a government that yearns to control each and every move we make. No other country in the world, at this point in time, would have the need or the desire to construct such a monstrosity to confine its own citizens.

The photograph below illustrates the dominance of this edifice in the Pittsburgh skyline and helps us appreciate its

**Allegheny County Jail Complex, Pittsburgh, PA.- the taxpayers' Taj Mahal**

grotesque enormity. Cars in the foreground look like ants. The stick they are crossing is, ironically, the venerable Liberty Bridge. This prodigious structure dwarfs any church or school building in the entire city, save the Cathedral of Learning at the University of Pittsburgh.

Some facts and figures about this county jail are as astounding as they are illuminating. In 2004, jail staff expenditures were approximately 2.3 million dollars and this figure increased to 3.0 million dollars in 2005. Almost unbelievably, however, this expenditure was just for *overtime labor* (www.prisonlegalnews.org, Dec. 18, 2010)!

For another example, by 2009 the jail budget was a whopping $11,522,250. Fooled again? This was just the budget for the Jail *Medical Division*! Here is a rundown of all actual expenses in 2009:

| | |
|---|---|
| Personnel | $29,244,102 |
| Fringe Benefits | 10,202,991 |
| Services | 14,102,310 |
| Supplies | 864,500 |
| Materials | 172,600 |
| Repairs/Maint. | 204,500 |
| Minor Equipment | 57,500 |
| Medical | 11,522,250 |
| TOTAL | $66,370,753 |

*(Figures from Allegheny County Website)*

Some of the medical expenses could have been avoided had the county not hired Traci Wilson, who was employed as an LPN. Wilson employed her creative therapeutic skills as a jail nurse by supplying marijuana, tobacco, and cell phones to inmates and fornicating with one of the prisoners. She pleaded guilty on August 19, 2010 to a whole host of charges: Two ungraded Felony Counts of Delivery of a controlled substance, a Felony-2 Count under the Crimes Code of furnishing controlled substances to a prisoner, an ungraded Misdemeanor count of unlawful possession of contraband, an ungraded Misdemeanor count of unlawful possession of a controlled substance, and an ungraded Felony count of Institutional Sexual Assault. (Case No. 5338-2010 Allegheny County). She was sentenced to eighteen months jail time. LPN Wilson was the second nurse in 2010 to have smuggled in dope to yardbirds[10]. Drug smuggling by guards and former guards has resulted in several criminal indictments over the years. Is there some degree of irony in that we as a society are criminalizing people for possessing drugs on the street, and then placing them in prisons, but yet we cannot even patrol drug traffic inside our prisons?

Bear in mind that the millions in prison medical expenses have not been sufficient to prevent the contraction of MRSA inside the jail. Perhaps someone will suggest that more than just $11 million needs to be spent. In September 2007 two guards at the Allegheny County Jail were infected with MRSA, and over an eighteen-month period twenty guards had staph infections, including ten cases of MRSA. These same guards are let loose after prison stewardship to spread their infections among the general population.

The happenings in Allegheny County and other western Pennsylvania counties are a parallel pattern for what has occurred across the United States in the past three decades. It is a direct result of the courts relinquishing control over the criminal justice system to the politicians. Politicians look and sound great when they are tough on crime and they are putting criminals behind bars. Voting "families" subscribe to this rhetoric: when the evil and dangerous go to jail, families are protected. But is only the dangerous

---

10 WPXI.COM, March 10, 2010.

and evil going to jail? Examine the devastating effects of our queer fetish for incarceration—both economically and socially—which has made the United States of America the world champion jailer. We have earned the ignominious title "YARDBIRD USA."

# CHAPTER 6

# Merry Christmas, Kate! The Bizarre Saga Of Kate Soul

It was Memorial Day weekend 2009. The clerk at the liquor store in Mercer, Pennsylvania, reported that a lady left the premises without buying any booze because she had no money. The liquor store clerk called 911 to report the strange behavior and the clerk was able to identify the car of one Kate Soul. Up the street a block or so the city patrolman spotted the same car. Kate was trying to either access the ATM machine or pump gas, but in the judgment of the cop, Kate could do neither. She appeared confused.

Confounded by the intricacies of the ATM machine and/ or the gas-pumping instructions at the Country Fair alerted the cop to Kate's apparently intoxicated state. In short time Kate was on her way to an arrest for DUI. (She denied having consumed any alcoholic beverages and refused the Blood Alcohol test and field sobriety tests.) This refusal to take a blood test can be an "inference of guilt" or it could mean that the suspect just did not want to cooperate because he or she disagreed with the reason for the arrest. Kate had no money to fight any aspect of the case and pleaded guilty.

---

*Com. v. KH 917* Cr. 2009 (Mercer County)

As a second-time offender, Kate faced a mandatory term of imprisonment of ninety (90) days. She would lose her license for eighteen months for refusing the chemical test and another eighteen months for the DUI, to be served consecutively, i.e., a three-year license suspension.

The Judge permitted house arrest in lieu of her mandatory jail sentence for two reasons. First, because we had won the Faith Hopski case (Chapter 2) and the Judge could therefore avail himself of that option, and second, because of, in part, her psychiatric problems, which included, but were not limited to, severe panic attacks, anxiety disorder, agoraphobia, and claustrophobic issues, along with depression. She began her house arrest term on December 10.

People "suffering" from panic-type and related disorders, especially when they collect social security disability, always hit a nerve with me and many other taxpayers. While many people work all day in imperfect conditions, these people take medications and get paid to stay home to avoid panic situations? However, this panic disorder appears to have a physiological foundation, and is closely related to the agoraphobia disorder, which involves a fear of being left in a situation where no help is available (on a bridge or in a crowd), and there is nowhere to hide. It would be hard to fabricate such a fear and that leads a queer credence to it. Research has uncovered a linkage between agoraphobia and difficulties with spatial orientation. Individuals without agoraphobia are able to maintain balance by combining information from their vestibular system, their visual system, and their proprioceptive sense. A disproportionate number of agoraphobics have weak vestibular function and consequently rely more on visual or tactile signals. They may become disoriented when visual cues are sparse, as in wide open spaces, or overwhelming, as in crowds. Likewise, they may be confused by sloping or irregular surfaces. Compared to controls, in virtual reality studies, agoraphobics on average show impaired processing of changing audiovisual data[11]. Kate apparently received a legitimate diagnosis of this disease from a licensed physician.

She was a petite young lady (5'6" and 125 pounds), not yet forty, with very nice teeth. Kate would not hurt a fruit fly, and despite her questionable DUI stop, she was now

11 See: Yardley, L; Britton, J; Lear, S; Bird, J; Luxon, LM (1995 May), "Relationship between balance system function and agoraphobic avoidance," and *Behav Res Ther.* 33 (4): 435–9 ; and Jacob, RG Furman, JM, Durrant, JD; Turner, SM (1996), "Panic, agoraphobia, and vestibular dysfunction," *Am J Psychiatry* 153 (4): 503–512.

a convict under the watchful but incredibly powerful eye, ear, and nose of the Mercer County House Arrest Authority. There are many conditions of house arrest, but the only one relevant for now was the no-tolerance policy for testing positive for alcohol.

Her boyfriend came over on Christmas Eve 2009 and they were planning to go to Kate's parents for Christmas the next morning. That night they watched movies and ate popcorn. Kate woke up in the morning, coffee was made, and her boyfriend made her a bagel. She showered but apparently the popcorn salt flavor included some type of mushroom garlic compote and Kate rashly decided to use a gargle rinse to neutralize the foul taste and odor.

Shortly thereafter, Kate got her random call from the Electronic Monitoring Department at which time she must exhale into a remote Portable Breath Test Device. The device reports back to House Arrest whether or not it detects alcohol on the breath of the person on house arrest. Alas, the first reading was positive and several successive positive readings were recorded. The police and house arrest brigade stormed her residence just a few moments later and whisked her off to prison. Merry Christmas, Ms. Soul!

Kate sat among yardbirds in the county jail for six weeks before we were retained to prepare a motion to have her released back on to the house arrest program. Her father, a dour and concerned man, contacted me for legal work. He was wholly confounded as to why Kate was in jail when she got house arrest at her sentencing, and she was not enjoying any alcoholic beverages during this time period.

Much of the progress attained by her physicians over the past few months regarding her disorders was compromised as Kate faced the hecklers and dimwits behind and beyond the jail cells. It took two hearings and another six weeks for us to obtain a favorable result, and in the mean-time, this bizarre story played out as a brilliant illustration of how wrong our system has become.

Sometimes the most trivial and insignificant cases such as this one (except to Ms. Soul, of course) provide the best insight as to how our system is operating, because it is this type of case—not the sensational, marquis cases—which are more likely to be repeated over and over on a daily basis throughout the courts everywhere.

Kate denied consuming any alcoholic beverages. Her father went to her house late that morning and saw no evidence of alcoholic beverage containers or bottles of beer, wine, or booze. Kate's boyfriend testified that there was no alcohol whatsoever in the house or in the trash. He was a very credible witness, despite his obvious bias in favor of his girlfriend. Finally, and perhaps most importantly, the house arrest brigade representative testified that (a) she had no indicia of being intoxicated and (b) that they found no alcoholic containers in the residence when they shackled and removed a dumbstruck Kate.

The results of her breath test monitor were illustrative. For those not too familiar with the breath testing devices commonly used, they are at best an *estimate* of blood alcohol levels in individuals being tested. They measure alcohol on the breath, not in the blood. A conversion factor based on Henry's Law translates the breath alcohol concentration to blood and a cookie-cutter formula is used to do this. A direct test on blood is more accurate, but even these tests are prone to error. Typically, one drink per hour (12 oz. beer, 4 oz. wine, or a mixed drink) in a normal 180 pound male will yield a Blood Alcohol level of .02 percent. In the same size individual, about .02 percent of Blood Alcohol Concentration is removed from the blood by respiration, perspiration, and liver function. Obviously, a petite individual will absorb more alcohol in one drink and will remove the same alcohol more slowly than a fatter peer. And my suspicions were that Kate's liver was by no means lily pink, but on the contrary had handled more than its share of effluvia over the years. This would make the tired old organ work even slower in removing the alcohol from the blood stream.

It should be remembered that the monitors used by House Arrest supervisors are below the standards of accuracy compared to the instruments used by the police. These remote devices are not approved for testing a suspect in a criminal prosecution, yet they can be used to remove someone from house arrest and incarcerate them in a prison, an oversight that seems to escape many people involved in the system, including Judges.

Kate's reported BAC test results are insightful.

| December 25 | Time | B.A.C. |
|---|---|---|
| | 8:34 a.m. | .058 % |
| | 8:53 | .049 |
| | 9:05 | .047 |
| | 9:23 | .042 |
| | 9:46 | .035 |

I argued cogently that these results were not consistent with alcoholic beverage consumption because the dissipation of alcohol was so rapid for a small person, particularly a female taking several potent medications, which are ultimately broken down in the liver. This young lady would most likely eliminate alcohol very slowly, not at the rate of .023 percent in slightly over an hour. Such an elimination rate on a tiny young woman taking medications would suggest some type of super liver when the more likely scenario would be a liver quite beaten down and forgotten. The Judge was experienced in these issues, which was very helpful, but he found enough evidence for "probable cause" of a violation, which mandated the detention of Kate. He ordered a full hearing, which is tantamount to a trial, on the issue of whether house arrest terms were violated.

At the full hearing on January 14, and after testimony and argument, the Judge found Kate in violation of House Arrest Conditions, and she was kept in prison. What was the reason for the detention of Ms. Soul? Even if she was not drinking, the rules of house arrest do not permit an arrestee to use any mouthwash since most mouthwashes contain alcohol and could flummox the results of the breath test. Thus, even if she convinced the Judge that she was not drinking alcoholic beverages, she would still face the possibility of jail since she had technically violated the rules of house arrest, which indirectly require that you maintain stinky breath by avoiding mouthwashes. The whole thing seems weird and wrong.

Finally, on February 17, 2010, after filing another motion (for reconsideration and rotation to house arrest), the Judge agreed that Kate could go back on the House Arrest Program. He did this reluctantly, but Kate was discharged from prison after nearly two months of confinement, still never having hurt anything or anyone and even providing some amusement to a stupid liquor store sales mullet. Perhaps the worst thing was that much of the progress made by her physicians to treat her various debilitating disorders had been wrecked by her term as a Mercer County Prison yardbird.

Kate's travails illustrate why we can never rely on house arrest or other half-assed programs to solve the prison population crisis. These programs are all administered by bureaucrats who have no concept of the big picture. House Arrest Coordinators make their jobs easier by having people thrown in jail. If everyone complied with the terms of their house arrest, there would be no need for their jobs as monitors.

House Arrest Coordinators also make the Judge's job easier and the Judge doesn't want to hear about the case after they have imposed their sentence. The House Arrest Coordinators are an arm of the court. The Judge wants the House Arrest people to deal with the defendant, and rightfully so. If the defendant violates the rules of House Arrest, and the House Arrest Coordinators bring it to the attention of the Judge, the defendant goes to jail. Period. The Judges will ALWAYS back the House Arrest Coordinators who are administering a program that makes the Judiciary's job easier. I have never seen a situation where a Judge has challenged one of their findings and I have even seen situations where these people have made mistakes so obvious that they have had to admit it, but the Defendant has already been incarcerated.

This places too much power in the hands of House Arrest Coordinators or other similar administrators of partial confinement programs. These individuals essentially perform the role of Judge if they charge a violation. They simply do not have the disposition, education, or experience in criminal law to such profound calls that potentially bemanure the lives and reputations of so many individuals.

Worse, these programs frequently turn into revenue sources for the government. As such, they carry with them all of the baggage of any other bureaucracy—the stubborn inaccessibility, the dimwitted responses to any situation other than the routine, the self-perpetuating mentality, the fat. As a branch of the Judiciary, they run hand in hand with the Judges to control sentenced defendants as easily and expensively as possible.

# CHAPTER 7

# Long and Soft—
# The Madoff Mentality

Mandatory prison sentences and the government's over-use of imprisonment do not translate into a theory that the conditions in our prisons are abhorrent, or cruel, or unjust. On the contrary, our modern prisons are quite comfy: air conditioning, cable television, recreation rooms, libraries, three square meals a day. Most prisons, even at the county level, have courses for inmates to work on their GED or substance abuse issues, and at the state level there is all-out vocational training. (Some classes, however, are required for parole, such as sex offender classes. These programs may be helpful and may just be another stumbling block on the way back to freedom.) In short, there may be an inverse relationship between soaring prison population and harsh prison conditions. When we see prisons take on the aura of a YMCA, that should be a signal that we have too many people in the system, and many people who do not belong there.

History supports this observation. The infamous Spanish Inquisition, dating back to the seventeenth century, teaches us that lenient prison conditions signify that people are serving terms of incarceration that probably are not justified. Early on in the Inquisition process heretics were burned. Decades later, heretics were punished for reading inappropriate materials, preaching inappropriately, and assembling inappropriately. The inquisition was politicized.

Inquisitorial prisons were some of the finest in Europe. Royal or ecclesiastical prisoners were known to have deliberately committed heretical crimes in order to be transferred to the upscale gaols of the Inquisition. Even then torture was acknowledged as a bogus way to obtain confessions due to the obvious taint and pressure. One prisoner, Miguel de la Pinta Llorente, was able to procure oil, vinegar, ice, eggs, chocolate, and bacon[12]. In today's prison this would translate to ProActiv acne care, an iPad, sausage McMuffins, oxys, and perhaps a gluteal tattoo of a safari animal.

In the nineteenth century, Louis Napoleon, nephew of Napoleon Bonaparte, was imprisoned for six years after a farcical attempt to overthrow the French Crown. Louis had two rooms, the company of two old friends, a mistress, a valet, and a dog, uncensored correspondence, access to a library, and other neat amenities[13].

As we will see later, many of our non-common law crimes have political and bureaucratic roots. And as we continue to attempt to regulate and monitor every aspect of each other's lives, more and more conduct will be criminalized through the political process. And while we will not have the stomach to torture or abuse prisoners running afoul of an oppressive government, the political process will call for incarceration to make its statement.

The real deterrent of jail is the loss of freedom and dignity: being forced to submit to the will of a jail guard; following rules, the sole purpose of which is to make the lives

---

12 The Spanish Inquisition, Henry Kamen, LCCC# 66-17728 (1965) pp. 172-173.
13 Louis Napoleon and the Second Empire, J.M. Thompson (1955), p. 72.

and times of jail wardens simple; enduring the uncertainty of when one will be released and what pieces of one's life will remain on the outside at that time. But these fears and apprehensions are very much subjective. Although they may take a great toll on the life of an intelligent and productive citizen, they have almost no effect upon the dullard or the dreg. All the cushy and expensive benefits tend to soften this blow to the pride of an intelligent human being confined to a pen with relatively less freedom than an animal in a modern zoo. But for the ignoramus with no hope or care in life, they simply make jail a decent place to live for a while. Warm, comfortable, three squares a day, and cable.

Louis Napoleon, despite the wonderful accommodations he enjoyed in prison, along with the protection and security in turbulent times, escaped from his confinement after six years of his life term. He later became the second Emperor of France. The human soul and hubris does not take well to being penned up and spoon fed, and always desires freedom to act on ambitions and dreams. Even a dimwitted beast will escape its cage if given the opportunity.

Much shorter jail sentences without the benefit of first class frills like air-conditioned gymnasiums, libraries, cable television, and fine desserts would be much more effective and much less costly punishment than the extraordinarily long, soft terms presently imposed. We should also take a closer look at permitting work release and other privileges that make confinement secondary to employment. This is a second, smaller part of the solution.

Surely, a judge without the constraints of sentencing guidelines could have fashioned a more appropriate sentence to convicted investment swindler Bernie Madoff than U.S. District Judge Denny Chim's sentence of 150 years in prison. This sentence, imposed on the seventy-one-year-old fraud, was nothing but pandering to the press and victims, an overkill statement lacking any originality (*USA v. Madoff* 09-213 in U.S. District Court for the Southern District of New York).

Madoff should have been given a six-month sentence where he was forced to live in a cardboard box under a dirty viaduct in the Bronx. He would be fed ordinary meals such as the common person in that area eats: dishwater soups, stale bread, rubber pasta, cereal that tastes like sand. Parched from panhandling, he would swill a glass of lemonade only to be fooled in that the glass contained nothing more than warm-colored water. He would bite into a fancy taco but fall victim to the cruel fraud that the seasoned meat was actually cold soil. He would almost starve, but not quite. He would receive a double CD of J.S. Bach's Brandenburg Concertos to play on his portable boom box only to find that the music was a compilation of duets with Wallace Beery and Hillary Clinton. He would continually be tricked, defrauded, and swindled until his head was spinning. Then, he would be released on parole under the supervision of the Securities and Exchange Commission where his talents for treachery and investment fraud would be utilized by the agency that could not detect his base criminal scheme. For their own shameful derelictions, members of the SEC would be forced to smell Madoff's nasty breath during all consultations.

A Centre County, Pennsylvania Court (home of Penn State University) was not to be outdone by Judge Denny Chim in the case of *Commonwealth v. Prisk* (22 Pa. Super. 2011; no. 846 MDA 2010). In this case, the sentence of child rapist Gary E. Prisk to a term of 633 to 1,500 years imprisonment was held to be within statutory guidelines by an appellate court. Prisk, aged fifty-six, was convicted by a jury of over three hundred counts of sexual offenses and cruel assaults committed over a six-year period on his step-daughter. President Judge David E. Grine, the sentencing Judge, despite his education, experience, and a salary of about $150,000 per year, could come up with no more original or effective sentence than the absurd one handed down to Prisk, making the pervert a common yardbird, eligible for parole at age 690. Assuming that Prisk lives to be one hundred years old, the effect of Judge Grine's sentence was to impose a prison term of 589 to 1,454 years upon a carcass.

Interestingly, this Prisk was in jail on an unrelated offense during a portion of the time he was raping. Prisk was permitted work release privileges during that soft sentence and utilized his work time slot to rape the infant victim on "almost a daily basis."

Short and harsh sentence terms, with some imagination sprinkled in, are a much less expensive manner of sentencing. Would this strategy be more effective than the long, mandatory, soft sentences now served by millions? But if the courts are shackled down in what they can do by the politicians, we get the absurd results presented here.

# CHAPTER 8

# Steve Highfoot: The Septuagenarian Yardbird

Mr. Steven Highfoot was a harmless seventy-two-year-old man who found himself in the Mercer County Jail for forty-five days in the spring of 2007. This elderly diabetic with no money did not fondle a schoolchild, punch a game warden, pistol whip a barber, or burn down a neighbor's garage. He toiled in the sun all day and then had a couple beers. Then he drove a vehicle.

On an unusually warm Memorial Day weekend in Northwestern Pennsylvania, Mr. Steven Highfoot drove up to his camp in Cochranton, PA, to get it ready for the summer. The tragic events occurred on May 27, 2006. Old man Highfoot cleaned out some of the buildings and loaded his pickup with four bags of outdated and outgrown toys. He did some maintenance around the property; cleaning, repairing windows, and then began to cut the grass. While mowing, he may have drunk two beers.

Just before dark he finished and began the journey home to McKees Rocks, PA, near Pittsburgh, about sev-

*Commonwealth v. SH,* No. 1177 Crim. 2006, Mercer County

enty-five miles away. He got hungry about a half hour into the trip and he stopped at a tavern Jackson Center, PA, for a sandwich. (There are no restaurants in Jackson Center, but at that time there were three taverns that served food as well as alcohol). Mr. Highfoot was not a wealthy man. And when he looked in his wallet his heart sank as he discovered he did not have enough money even for a sandwich, just for a draft beer or two. So that was his dinner.

Apparently, no one at the bar felt Mr. Highfoot was too impaired to drive, so he left the tavern without anyone noticing. He headed south on I-79. His life took a bum turn when a Pennsylvania State Trooper just happened to catch up to him and follow him with eagle eyes.

When Steven had got back on the Interstate in Jackson Center, some of the toys spilled out in the cab of the truck as he rounded the entry ramp. Highfoot tried to move these articles out of the driving area of the cab so they would not interfere with the operation of the vehicle (pedals), but when he was doing this, his vehicle crossed over the dotted center line of I-79. According to the Trooper, this happened six times in a half mile of travel (almost impossible, even at a reduced speed of 50 mph). Highfoot was traveling below the speed limit in the right lane of this four-lane highway and no other traffic was affected by his "erratic" driving. Nonetheless, the Trooper initiated a traffic stop and Highfoot slowly pulled over into a safe area off the road to accommodate the Trooper in his eventual arrest and prosecution.

According to Police, Highfoot reeked of beer. He was asked to exit the vehicle and do a series of field sobriety and tests (balance and dexterity), which he performed with all of the aplomb of a pig on ice. He was arrested on the berm of Interstate 79. He was taken for a blood alcohol test at the Grove City Medical Center and the result put him in the highest range under Pennsylvania's DUI statute (.205 percent according to Grove City Hospital lab).

Being that this was his second offense within ten years, Highfoot was facing a mandatory prison sentence of ninety days to five years, with an eighteen month driver's license suspension, a fine of $1,500, plus a tortuous walk through the bureaucracy that has grown like a fast-spreading cancer around the DUI post conviction process.(His first offense in 2000 could not have been serious either, as he was granted "ARD," a pre-trial diversionary program which allows an offender to earn dismissal of the charges and expungement of his record upon completing a probationary period. No one is eligible for this program if their DUI involved an accident with serious bodily injury). The mandatory parole period for the seventy-two-year-old man was a solid five years. If all went well, a cowering Highfoot could be released from the shackles of his parole officer just before his seventy-eighth birthday party.

What was unusual about this case, of course, was that this poor, seventy-two-year-old man with diabetes, and taking a 1000 mg. prescription dosage of Glipizide, was headed to jail to commingle with the thieves, molesters, drug addicts, and other DUI offenders. Under the mandatory sentencing laws, no account whatsoever is given to his age of seventy-two, the fact that he hurt no one, and his flawed medical condition. He was mandated by the legislature to go to jail for ninety days. The Judge actually exercised some degree of leniency by permitting a furlough after forty-five days to allow service of the final forty-five days of the mandatory prison term on house arrest. (At that time this was the way to circumvent the ninety-day mandatory jail time).

I would respectfully suggest that Mr. Highfoot's scenario is repeated time and time again in our country as a result of mandatory sentencing, particularly for DUI offenses. That is why it is somewhat difficult to make this chapter unique or compelling. I also suggest that no Judge in his right mind would incarcerate such a man if it were not because of mandatory sentence laws.

One of the most pathetic scenes I have ever had to witness was to visit Mr. Highfoot in the County Prison after his sentence, to discuss a sentence modification motion. He hobbled down the steps of his block, walking past the other inmates who were clucking at him stupidly, totally humiliated in his orange jump suit. This was a man who grew up in an era where the police would direct one home or to a hotel if one had too much to drink and if one was half decent to the cop. He lived in an era of respect where, if you didn't hurt anyone, there was no great need to hurt you. It was an era when old men didn't go to prison for swilling a few beers after cutting the grass. It was an era of common sense and decency, which has apparently passed us by.

We met in a private room and I felt sorry for the old lout. No one even knew how to play spades on his block. The food was awful and it was tough to get a cold beer. But he was simple enough, dim enough, and resilient enough to make it through the forty-five days of jail, and maybe prison "taught him a lesson," but if cooler heads actually prevailed, such a scenario would not be necessary.

# CHAPTER 9

# Nelson Candela— "This is Ridiculous"

Nelson Candela was a real estate broker, developer, and community spokesman. He graduated from Grove City College and eventually owned his own real estate firm. He came from a family of college graduates and had three brothers who succeeded in education and coaching. Mr. Candela also had a side profession as an interior designer. He was President of the Mercer County Industrial Authority. He worked to develop industrial parks in the Grove City and Wheatland area and residential areas such as Village Park in Grove City, where hundreds of beautiful homes have been built and millions of tax dollars have been generated. He also participated in organizations that opposed development that would clearly harm the communities he had worked so hard to build up, most notably the notorious Tri-County Landfill, which has attempted to bemanure all of southern Mercer County with a hideous landfill located right next to the Grove City Airport.

Experts like Mr. Candela were welcome when it was time to organize real estate progress, move properties, and

---

*Com. v. CMB* No. 1248 Crim. 2005 (Mercer County)
*Com. v. CMB* No. 1689 Crim. 2006 (Mercer County)

stop derogatory development. Overcoming the downsides of his divorce, the effects of depression and bipolar disorder, chronic halitosis, and a mild lisp, the idiosyncratic Candela was an important element in a declining County— Mercer County, Pennsylvania. His family situation and his occupation combined to place pressure on Candela and an alcohol issue oozed forward. But it would be hard for anyone who knew him well to believe that he had a serious alcohol problem.

It would be even harder for anyone to believe that Mr. Candela, at age sixty-six, would wind up spending several months in the hoosegow. Our prisons are full of boozers and dimwits—more so than serious criminals. Quite frequently, the prisons also catch more prominent and intelligent people who believe it impossible that "it could happen to them." Mr. Candela falls into this category of yardbird.

The problems started on May 8, 2003, when he was picked up for a Driving Under the Influence charge in Butler County, Pennsylvania. As a first-time offender, this case was easily resolved under the ARD program. So long as no one was seriously hurt in a wreck, and the offender possessed a valid driver's license, and he had no previous DUI offenses or other serious criminal record, he qualified for this disposition. There was no jail time, a year's probation, and a thirty-day license suspension. (I did not represent him on this case and therefore do not know any of the details of the alleged offense.)

The license suspension was to begin on April 26, 2004. For some reason, Mr. Candela did not receive his license back from Penn Dot, but after thirty days' service, he began to drive again. One of three things had to occur to account for this error, which would later compound into a lengthy visit to the Mercer County Prison. First, Candela could have failed to surrender his license when notified to do so by Penn Dot and therefore Penn Dot never began recording his thirty-day service of suspension. Second, Candela could have surrendered his license but not sent in his restoration card with the $25 restoration fee and therefore his license was never restored. Third, Penn Dot could have bungled the case. Knowing both Mr. Candela and his tendency to play fast and loose with those in authority, and knowing Penn Dot's bureaucratic imbecilities, the odds were about 33.33 percent for each of the above scenarios.

The groundwork for disaster was set, however. On October 24, 2004, Mr. Candela was pulled over again by the Po Po and it did not take them long to retrieve his Penn Dot record showing that he was still under suspension. Under the circumstances, he was able to plead guilty to Driving During Suspension, but not with the DUI suspension enhancement, which would have called for a MANDATORY ninety-day jail sentence [75 Pa.CSA 1543(b)]. However, any Driving During Suspension offense in Pennsylvania results in an additional one-year suspension of operating privileges. According to Penn DOT records, this suspension began on April 22, 2005, again lasting until April 21, 2006 if there were no additional intermittent violations.

But Nelson Candela was a Real Estate Broker and President of the Mercer County Industrial Development Authority. How would he get to all his appointments and social functions without driving a motor vehicle? The short answer to that rhetorical question is that he would not. He needed to drive to earn a livelihood and partake in community activities.

## Candela I

On June 18, 2005, Mr. Candela had attended a Realtor's function in Cranberry Township, PA, about an hour away from his home, now in Hermitage, Mercer County. He had taken aboard four or more glasses of wine and proceeded north on Interstate 79. He made it forty miles to the interchange with Interstate 80 without any problem. Then he proceeded west to the Hermitage exit, another twenty-five miles. He had not wrecked into a tree or a dumpster, and had not run over a small child in leukemia remission. But when he got three blocks from his home on Pine Hollow Boulevard, he ran into Officer Daniel Best of the Hermitage Police Department.

Officer Best was a green cop who did not even have a year's experience under his belt. But he was learning the ropes quickly. On June 18, 2005, he was stationed at the now-defunct Jai Alai Bar on Mercer Road at closing time. He admitted to sitting there to observe traffic and "for purposes of catching people driving under the influence of alcohol." He testified that he saw headlights coming down the road and a white Cadillac straddling the yellow line. The vehicle made a left onto Pine Hollow Boulevard at the light. Best pulled behind the vehicle and followed it along Pine Hollow Boulevard. The vehicle was traveling at a safe speed, about thirty miles per hour, and there were no other vehicles in sight. The vehicle was consistently across the yellow line, a technical violation of the motor vehicle code, so Best initiated a traffic stop after following and observing his driving for about a mile and half. Mr. Candela pulled his vehicle over in a safe spot, at a parking lot, in a fairly prompt manner.

It annoyed Officer Best that Candela got out of his vehicle simultaneously with the kid cop. "You are not to get out of the vehicle unless directed to do so by the officer," young Best puffed. I asked him where he got that idea and he stated it was "procedure." I asked him if he ever told Mr. Candela to "stay seated in his car," and Officer Best said no, he did not. Candela admitted to the young Officer of having no license and stated he had just driven from Pittsburgh and was three blocks from home. Best could have cared less. He noticed bloodshot and watery eyes and mumbled speech. Best then began a battery of field sobriety tests to pad his case. He started with the ABCs, which, according to Best, was a failure by Candela as he ignored all letters from Q to W each of the three times he attempted the test. Next were some dexterity tests, which combine elements of both ballroom dancing and yoga: finger touch nose with eyes closed, standing on one leg motionless while counting to thirty, and the notorious "walk and turn" test—walking nine steps in a straight line, pirouetting, and returning another nine steps gloriously to the precise starting point. After abysmal performances, as graded by Officer Best, Mr. Candela was told he was under arrest for DUI.

"No, don't do this," he pleaded, to no avail. Steadfastly, Officer Best placed the handcuffs on the sixty-six-year-old Candela's left hand and Mr. Candela took his right hand to grab Best's arm and plead once more, "Don't do this." Best threatened him, "Mr. Candela, let go of my arm. I don't want this to get physical. You are under arrest." When Candela failed to allow Best to cuff his right arm, Best put him in an arm bar and placed him over the hood of the car, again asking Candela for his right hand to cuff. (Candela would state that the cuffs were excruciatingly tight on his left wrist and that was the issue in saying "please don't do this." Best denied that he heard complaints about the pain of the cuffs but did admit that it is a frequent cry among arrestees.)

Candela pushed away from the cruiser and Best goose-necked his left arm, taking him to the ground hard. Candela's glasses were shattered and his face was cut open as he gave up his right hand to the all-powerful and mighty Best for the handcuffs. Best then transported the cowed Candela to the Sharon Regional Health System for a Blood Alcohol analysis. Candela readily consented to the test. He gave no lab personnel any problem. He was not belligerent in any way to anyone except Officer Best. This, too, is a common scenario, and when the cop is repeatedly in these situations, you have to wonder who, in fact, is provoking or baiting the behavior that is eventually charged to the Defendant in the form of Resisting Arrest charges.

Candela's blood alcohol level came back at .157 per cent, almost twice the legal limit but much lower than many DUI offenders. In fact, he was just under the .16 threshold, which carries more serious penalties. He was also charged with resisting arrest and some traffic violations, the most serious being driving during DUI suspension—a killer offense, as mentioned above, with the ninety-day mandatory jail sentence. It is interesting to note that the original charge was technically incorrect, charging Candela with driving under a DUI suspension based upon the repealed DUI statute instead of the newly enacted statute. I argued that the charge, as filed, was a nullity and should be quashed, but the Commonwealth was not only allowed to amend its complaint and correct the charge it was permitted to add the enhancement for Driving During Suspension with greater than .02 alcohol in system, which increases the mandatory jail time from sixty to ninety days.

We clearly had an uphill battle defending Mr. Candela. One of the biggest problems was that under the DUI statute, as interpreted then, a Defendant is not entitled to a jury trial[14]. In other words, the government need only convince a judge, rather than twelve jurors unanimously, that they have met their burden of proof beyond a reasonable doubt. In my experience, Judges tend to employ a "sufficiency of evidence" test in trials rather than the "reasonable doubt"

---

14 We presently have a case on appeal arguing that a DUI defendant has enough at stake with the criminal penalties, the mandatory counseling, fines, and operator's license suspensions, that denial of a jury trial is a violation of Article 6 to the Pennsylvania Constitution.

standard. The District Attorneys usually have their way with the trial judges in bench trials for this reason.

We filed a suppression motion arguing that there was not probable cause for the stop of the vehicle. This motion was heard on February 8, 2006 and, within minutes thereafter, was denied, and we proceeded to the bench trial.

We stipulated with the Commonwealth that they could use the testimony of the officer at the Suppression hearing, rather than have him come in and re-testify. We also stipulated to the Blood Alcohol Test procedures and results. From our standpoint, the only way to win the case was on appeal of the ruling that the traffic stop was legal. Once he failed the field sobriety tests and tested at .157 within two hours of driving, our ship was sunk, particularly in front of a judge rather than a jury. It made no sense to spend the time and money on a full-blown trial when the only hope was a reversal of the previous ruling on the traffic stop. A defendant in this rather common tactical situation cannot simply plead guilty, however. He must go through a trial, even if by stipulated facts, in order to preserve his appeal issue on the traffic stop.

The trial was scheduled for March 16, 2006 before the presiding Judge. I would like to say it was a brilliant defense tactic that led to the result that followed, but it was, in reality, blind luck. By stipulating to the previously given testimony of the officer on the issue of the traffic stop, the Commonwealth was left with no evidence whatsoever on the Resisting Arrest charge! This rather serious charge was withdrawn just prior to the entry of a demurrer, which would have had the same effect as the withdrawal. The bad, but inevitable news, however, was that Nelson Candela was pronounced guilty of Driving Under the Influence and Driving During Suspension, DUI-related, by the Judge just seconds after the last witness had climbed down out of the witness box.

Sentencing was originally scheduled for May 30, 2006 and was postponed until June 8, 2006. Candela received the mandatory minimums of thirty days for the DUI and ninety days for the Driving During DUI Suspension. Again, the court had no discretion to impose any lesser sentence even if it wished to do so. Mandatory fines were $750 and $1000 respectively. Many other provisions were ordered as part of the sentence, but at some point, we as lawyers and as readers must be spared of the details which attend each and every DUI case, much as a stray dog eventually ignores the whines of the nasty neighbor trying to protect his garbage can.

The court docket in this case covered nineteen pages. There were perhaps more court orders (I counted twenty two) entered in this case than any other ungraded misdemeanor in world history. Furloughs, continuances, evaluations, motions on the merits of the case, detainers, Gagnons, motions to revoke house arrest and motions for contempt for failure to pay fines and costs. The total court costs and fines to Mr. Candela for this DUI in which there was no accident, no injury, and where he was stopped just blocks from his garage, was $8,258.50. That did not include fees for his lawyer. A judgment for this amount was entered against him as a matter of course and collection efforts by way of contempt proceedings were repeatedly brought against this clearly beaten down Defendant. The County of Mercer was proving itself one of the most litigious parties in all of Western Pennsylvania. The costs of prosecuting this case, housing and transporting Mr. Candela included, were astronomical. And although this may be an extreme case in this regard, it is certainly not beyond that which occurs regularly in our judicial system.

## Candela II

On September 21, 2006, Mr. Candela attended a realtor's dinner at the now-defunct Sharon Country Club. After the dinner, he saw an old and good friend over in another room having dinner with his now-divorced wife. He was invited to join, and took aboard two glasses of fine wine. He left for Jesse's restaurant just three or four miles away to meet another realtor on a deal they were working on. He had only club soda there. His next stop was in nearby Sharpsville, another three or four miles away, to pick up some more papers.

All was well until Officer Matthew C. Sharp noticed a gold Lincoln traveling the wrong way on a one-way street. That Lincoln was, of course, the vehicle operated by Mr. Candela. Officer Sharp stopped the vehicle, which had turned west onto West Ridge Road. The officer detected the odor of alcoholic beverages about Mr. Candela's vehicle and noticed glossy, bloodshot eyes. Mr. Candela admitted having taken on a glass of wine. Officer Sharp asked Candela to exit and perform four field sobriety tests, which were deemed failures by the arresting cop. Candela then refused to go to the hospital and submit to the blood alcohol test. For a seasoned DUI defendant and college graduate, this was the opposite tactic to take. The field sobriety tests should always be refused because (a) there are no consequences for refusal, (i.e., they are totally optional), and (b) only a gymnast or NBA point guard could actually pass the tests to the satisfaction of an arresting DUI cop. On the contrary, the blood alcohol test should almost always be taken since (a) failure to submit to the test results in an automatic one year license suspension (in PA and most other states), (b) failure to submit to the test can be argued as consciousness of guilt in the trial, and (c) the blood test result can always be challenged later if it comes up extraordinarily high. The only time to refuse the test is if there is an accident with a fatality or serious injury and no evidence at all should be offered by the defendant as to his own condition.

But there was more for Mr. Candela. According to Sharp, "Upon telling Candela that he was under arrest for DUI and requesting that he put his hands behind his back, Candela refused." The backup officer also advised Candela to comply or force would be used to make him comply. Candela then "tensed up his arms in refusal to be arrested." The backup officer took Candela to the back of the vehicle to restrain his arms and place him under arrest. "At that time the backup officer received an injury to his shoulder, which he was treated for at the local hospital." Candela was charged with his second consecutive Resisting Arrest concomitant with a DUI, perhaps the only Grove City College graduate in history to attain this distinction.

Yet the comedy of errors continued, as everyone involved in these cases except me continued to bungle them. At the preliminary hearing, the backup officer who was injured failed to appear and testify. I argued that the arresting officer could not testify as to the injury of his fellow officer and the magistrate agreed. Without the injury, the Resisting Arrest allegation carried little muster as it merely involved an elderly gentleman unhappy about being faced with another DUI charge and putting up nominal physical resistance, which is, to some degree, expected in any arrest. The magistrate tossed out the Resisting Arrest charge after the preliminary hearing.

The Mercer County Common Pleas Court issued a detainer on Mr. Nelson Candela. This is an insidious court order, which typically follows a report by a parole officer that the parolee has violated his conditions of parole by committing another criminal offense. Even though such allegations have not been proven at all, the mere arrest of a parolee triggers the detainer order and the defendant sits in yardbird city until his case is disposed of or other terms of release are negotiated.

The detainer was issued September 27, 2006 and was followed up by a Court Order on October 6, 2006 directing Candela be incarcerated and evaluated for Drug and or Alcohol issues. On December 14, 2006, Mr. Candela was rotated from the County Jail into house arrest as part of the detainer. He was permitted to work and be counseled. Not until October 10, 2007 was Mr. Candela released from House Arrest, on grounds that he had completed his treatment. His 2006 DUI offense was still unresolved at that time. He spent eighty-two days in prison and nearly another ten months on house arrest.

What happened at his second DUI trial was once again a magnificent waste of resources and comedy of errors. A jury of twelve was sworn in on September 19, 2007. Since Candela refused the chemical test, the government had no proof of a level of intoxication. They had to rely on the driving itself to show impairment, as well as the officer's trained observations of intoxication. The officer did not make a good witness. We called witnesses who saw Mr. Candela right before he left for Sharspville who contradicted the officer's conclusions. We also showed photographs of the scene of the one-way road where Mr. Candela had pulled out onto West Ridge Street from the parking lot of the bowling alley and the DO NOT ENTER sign indicating a one-way street was not visible to a motorist when pulling out from that particular point. The District Attorney's suggestion that the sixty-six-year-old President of the Mercer County Industrial Authority actually went out to the scene and twisted the sign did not apparently go over very well with the jury. But the result was not an acquittal. After three days of trial, the jury reported that it was hopelessly deadlocked and a mistrial was declared on September 21, 2007. It was learned that the split was a near unanimous 11-1 in favor of acquittal. Under Pennsylvania Law, the Judge ruled on the summary offenses, not the jury. The trial Judge's verdict was (surprise) that Mr. Candela was Guilty of Driving Without a License, Guilty of Driving Down a One-Way Street, and Guilty of Driving Under DUI-related Suspension with Alcohol in System, the big one carrying the mandatory ninety-day jail term and $1,000 fine.

Normally stubborn with DUI cases, the District Attorney simply lists any DUI mistrial for a re-trial the next term of court. But given the overwhelming vote for acquittal and perhaps getting a bit worn down in the process as well, we were offered a plea bargain. It was an offer we could not refuse in that the Judge put on the record that he would not impose any more jail time. Candela pleaded No Contest to DUI under the general impairment section. The enhancement for refusal, which placed this in a one-year mandatory sentencing matrix, was dropped. In other words the potential jail time dropped from one to five years to ten days to two years. In addition, Candela faced the Driving Under Suspension charge, which could run concurrently or consecutively to the DUI. The plea occurred on December 10, 2007.

The sentence on February 8, 2008 was anticlimactic, or at least should have been. The Judge imposed the mandatory ten days for the DUI, plus the fine of $500, giving him credit for sixty days time served from October 17, 2006 to December 15, 2006 and releasing him that date under parole, for a total of one year and six months. Weirdly, the Judge forgot to sentence Candela on the Driving Under DUI Suspension and other summary offenses. Perhaps this was because it was part of the verdict in the first trial, not the subsequent plea, and was lost in time. Rather than go back and re-sentence Mr. Candela when the error was caught, the Judge vacated the convictions on all the summary offenses. This saved Mr. Candela several thousand dollars and potentially ninety more days in jail, plus makes him eligible for license restoration one year earlier than he would otherwise have been—a huge break due less from nifty legal representation than systematic bungling.

But there was one more botch to occur in the saga.

## Candela III

In the fall of 2010, about three years after all his court cases had concluded, but whilst still under the watchful eye of his counselors, probation officers, and family, Mr. Candela appeared at a college alumni reunion at the Country Club (a country club Mr. Candela was forced to resign from after decades of membership, due to his financial woes). Here, the mistakes made in his case were compounded by yet another foible.

It was a jovial evening and the crowd around the bar was thick. The bartender was a newly hired brunette who wore tight-fitting under armor now that fall had chased summer off. She was very attractive but had not yet honed all the skills a club manager might desire from a barmaid in the practice of mixology. Mr. Candela calmly ordered an "Old Fashioned" beverage and chatted with friends from years gone by while he waited. He reached for his drink, sipped it clandestinely, and continued mingling. Much to his consternation, however, the barmaid had not served him an Old Fashioned at all, but instead unwittingly had proffered a "Shirley Temple." Candela's colleagues eventually noticed the gaffe at about the same time that he did, and Mr. Candela was clearly not amused.

I would guess that this precise mixological *faux pas* had occurred before sometime in the history of mankind, but never under the circumstances herein set forth. Here we have a proud and successful graduate of the college returning for the reunion, but with the stain of an alcohol-related record. Some of those present may know about the legal/ alcohol problems; others would not. He orders a drink in spite of it all, maybe to show those interested that there is no problem and he was master of his own beverage decisions. Yet the drink that comes before him and is showcased in the eyes of his peers is none other than a Shirley Temple—the same drink that might be requested by his eight-year-old granddaughter at Appleby's after the Dairy Queen is closed.

Such moments are priceless. As it applied to Mr. Candela, the only scenario comparable to this shocking episode might be if, after several months of wallowing in the darkness of the county prison, Mr. Candela finally achieves his day of release. On a summer morning, he leaps through the prison doors towards his freedom only to find that the sky has been blackened by a total solar eclipse and the only light in view is from the flames engulfing his lonely white Cadillac, parked in the prisoner's lot.

After a couple sips of the Shirley Temple, a crestfallen Mr. Candela remarks to no one in particular, "This is ridiculous." Whether he is speaking of just that moment in time, or the last five years of his life, I could not agree more.

# CHAPTER 10

# Joe Smith: Masturbation = Incarceration

Joe Smith was your average Joe. Until 2007. He was born in western Pennsylvania in July of 1961 and grew up in a normal family environment with two brothers and parents who had been married over fifty years. Joe's childhood was normal with no reported abuse or neglect. He graduated from high school with average credentials and served in the Army during the tail end of the Jimmy Carter presidency. At that time, America's worst president* wrecked our economy and western Pennsylvania was one of the weakest areas. Joe Smith had nothing to keep him here at age eighteen. Carter had troops all over the globe trying to plug holes in a floundering foreign policy and Joe Smith wound up stationed in Europe. Smith's soldierly conduct there involved binge boozing and brothels where he fornicated with several dozen whores. No one could know at the time, but this behavior heralded his future. Smith was Honorably Discharged after four years at the rank of Sergeant.

---

*Commonwealth v. DDS* CP-37-CR-1084 and 1090-2007 Lawrence County

* America's best president, according to the head of the history department at my alma mater, Grove City High School, was William Henry Harrison, who contracted pneumonia during his inauguration in 1841 and died one month after taking office.

Jack W. Cline

The military manners carried over to his civilian days as a truck driver whence he utilized the services of an occasional prostitute while alone on the road. He reportedly exposed himself to female passersby as part of his truck driving regimen. Smith was married in 1988 at age twenty-seven. Within the marriage, sex was common at first but quickly ran into the law of diminishing returns. Actual copulation gradually gave way to masturbation. But the marriage lasted eleven years, ending in a divorce in 2000. The couple bore a daughter who, unfortunately, was groped and molested by the ex-wife's new boyfriend. The boyfriend pled guilty to Corruption of Minors and Endangering the Welfare of Children in Beaver County in 2005. But Child Services removed Joe's daughter from the home because the ex-wife continued to allow the perverted paramour back into the residence.

After the divorce in 2000, Smith acquired an out-of-town girlfriend who was nine years younger than he. This in itself may not have been weird, but the fact that the two worked on masturbation technique more than intercourse, taking the practice to great heights, may have been considered somewhat unusual.

So it was not a Normal Rockwell portrait of an American boy, but at the same time it was far from a bizarre life. Joe Smith had no juvenile record and no adult criminal record. He eventually owned his own home in Ellwood City, Pennsylvania. He had excellent credit and was now, by 2007, working for Ryerson (a metal production company) as a crane operator. He has no serious physical, medical, or mental health conditions.

Smith was, however, developing a shine to young women and girls, but clearly in a masturbation context[15].

---

15 The word "masturbation" is believed by many to derive from a plural Greek word for penis (μεζεα—mezea) and the Latin verb turbare, meaning to disturb. A competing etymology derivation is based on a Latin expression manus turbare meaning "to disturb with the hand" and is regarded by most dictionaries as "an old conjecture." Source: WordIQ.com.

In January, 2007, Smith jumped into an online chat room with various people. One of them was a thirteen-year-old girl named Brianna. Brianna had posted pictures and Smith commented that she looked like eighteen, not thirteen years of age. The conversation moved quickly from small talk to sexual preferences. Smith then proceeded to give Brianna an online lesson in vaginal masturbation, setting forth a step-by-step failsafe procedure. A frenetic Smith turned on his webcam and he himself masturbated for Brianna online—not one of the more wholesome uses of the internet as contemplated by its creator, the hon. Al Gore.

Smith stated that he wished he could "do it" (masturbate) to her. He initiated a chat two days later, which was essentially a repeat of the previous lesson, with some additional counsel and guidance. He then sent an online picture of a young girl masturbating to illustrate his chapter lesson. Nothing happened that we know of for a month or so and on February 20, 2007 a third chat was initiated.

Brianna told Smith she had not been practicing the masturbation techniques he had so meticulously outlined. Small talk ensued about Joe dating Brianna's mom so all three could get together. The fourth chat was another month later and was more specific as to Smith's desire to have oral sex with Brianna, referring to the picture online and stating that he lived only a half hour away from her. Two innocuous chats occurred, then a chat on April 6 highlighting the joys of masturbation once again. Three more chats resulted in Smith giving out his cell phone number and soliciting text messages. The immaturity of such conversations—"I miss u," "hi sexy girl how did you get so sexy?"—was astounding, even for an Army sergeant.

Brianna baited the horned up sergeant, asking, "Where we would engage in such sexual situations?" to which he replied, "I don't know . . . I'd get into big trouble if we got caught." Another chat in May covered more intimate topics concerning the sexual organ of Mr. Smith and how to take care of it, this conversation occurring by texting on the cellular phone. Finally, Smith made the bold suggestion that they get together when school was out.

A second thirteen-year-old, "Jenna," appeared in Smith's chat room. Smith viewed her online profile (photos) and made such infantile comments as "u r gorgeous." He also stated "if u were 18. . . I'd be wanting to meet u!" and "much as I want to . . . I just can't take the chance sweety . . . I hope u understand . . . I mean . . . u really make me horny . . . ur that beautiful . . . etc." Did Smith really have any intent to contact or molest the thirteen-year-old flirts? Or were they just masturbation fodder?

Conversations continued through June and the masturbation juices flowed online and off. Webcam evidence would prove that Smith could, in fact, masturbate repetitively before a camera. Brianna continued the conversations, the goading. "U r so sexy and I really want to taste your but I just (sic) chance it."

Despite his acknowledged reticence, Smith continued the chats, up to twenty now, and wanted to meet Brianna in his swimming pool to engage in masturbatory acts, including oral sex. In the last conversation, Sergeant Smith worked himself into a lather: "I want to swim naked with you sooo bad. It's been so long since I've made love to a woman. . . . I wish we could be together for a while. . . . id love to take you with me if I move . . . I would treat you like my little princess! Anything you wanted & we could play around all the free time we had."

At this point, Brianna had had enough. Did she tell him to stop, that it was going too far? No. Did she tell her dad? No again. Did she report it to a school executive or a counselor? None of those. In fact, she applied for an arrest warrant before the District Justice, charging Mr. Joe Smith,

Army Sergeant and regular American, with four counts of Unlawful Contact with a Minor and four counts of Criminal Use of a Communication Facility. Brianna also applied for a search warrant of Smith's residence with authority to seize his computer, web cam, other electronic devices, and any photos in his house. How did Brianna know where he lived? She had obtained authority to apply to Yahoo for the purpose of obtaining the identity of Mr. Smith's online user ID in the chat room.

It turns out, naturally, that there was no Brianna, or Jenna. Brianna was fake bait, created online by a Special Agent for the Office of the Attorney General in Commonwealth of Pennsylvania. Bedroom Cop Dan Osinski had created a crime, and if it were up to him, Joe Smith was going to jail.

We should step back for a moment and analyze the crimes code. Having consensual sexual activity and making payment to your partner is a criminal offense (Prostitution 18 P.S. Section 5902). Having *sex per os* (meaning, by mouth, as in fellatio or cunnilingus) is deviate sexual intercourse (18 P.S. 3101), as is the use of any digit (finger or toe) in foreplay, and as is *sex per anus* (sodomy). Vaginal sex is still not criminal so long as it is free, and penis goes directly into vagina. The missionary position is highly recommended to avoid any risk that the government would mistake the activity for *per anus* penetration, and for further safety, the anus should probably be taped over with an opaque adhesive. This would minimize the risk that such conduct could be deemed sodomatic. It is important to understand that masturbation is legal only if the actor is dreaming about his spouse, girlfriend, or neighbor's spouse. It is criminal if the actor flashes a thought about a child under eighteen, a unicorn, or a whore. The law is unclear at the present time as to the use of cartoon images, so these too should be avoided until the legislatures take a

81

firm position. Bear in mind that this advice is not typically proffered by sexual therapists, marriage counselors, or other under educated professionals, but it is most definitely sound, if gratuitous, legal advice.

Special Agent Dan Osinski was assigned to duties associated with the Pennsylvania office of Attorney General Child Predator Unit of the Criminal Investigations and Prosecutions Section. His duties include the online undercover investigation of adult subjects who attempt to communicate with minors by use of a computer and who attempt to subsequently meet the minors in order to engage in sexual activity. Osinski adopted the undercover identities of the two minors, thirteen-year-olds "Brianna" and "Jenna." He created online profiles or pseudo-identities of these female children, which clearly identified them as thirteen-year-old girls. (This Osinski is now the lead investigator for the Cuyahoga County Prosecutor's Ohio ICAC Task Force, coordinating and supervising undercover online investigations involving child predators and child pornography. Osinski moved up in the chain of prosecution after he was employed as a special agent with the Pennsylvania Office of the Attorney General's Bureau of Criminal Investigation. He was responsible for more than sixty arrests throughout the United States and Canada involving online sexual exploitation of children and it is my suspicion that this phase of his career was merely a personal stepping stone for an agenda that involves more prestigious operations. He now fancies himself as an expert in "cyber bullying," speaking at various seminars on this nebulous topic).

The criminal charges lodged against Joe Smith were very serious. Under the Unlawful Contact With Minor Charges [18 Pa.C.S. 6315(a)(5)], each charge was a third-degree felony, carrying with it a maximum term of imprisonment of seven years. This set of charges was for masturbating to "Brianna" on the internet.

The last time I had looked, it was a defense to a criminal charge that the alleged crime was factually impossible. I remembered the old law school illustrations that there could be no crime or attempted crime when there was no subject of the criminal act. In other words, if an ashen-colored tree stump in the middle of a field takes on the precise image of the aged Pennsylvania Senator Arlen Specter, and a rabid fan of common decency holding a deer rifle decides that it is a perfect time to take the Senator out for the good of the cause, and the actor shoots the tree stump dead, then there can be no crime because, in fact, all the actor did was shoot a tree stump. It makes no difference that the shooter believed and wished that the stump was the pompous Senator. Applying that logic to this case, I believed we had a defense. Sgt. Smith, despite his longing to masturbate before the eyes of a thirteen-year-old girl, in fact only masturbated before the longing eyes of Agent Osinski, a consenting adult who was clearly "asking for it."

But alas the legislature pre-empted this time-honored principle of common law when the child abuse statute was enacted, stating as follows:

"A person commits an offense if he is intentionally in contact with a minor, or a law enforcement officer acting in the performance of his duties who has assumed the identity of a minor, for the purpose of engaging in an activity under any of the following, and either the person initiating the contact or the person being contacted is within this Commonwealth: (1) Any of the offenses enumerated in Chapter 31 (sexual offenses), (2) Open Lewdness, (3) Prostitution, (4) Obscene and other sexual materials and performances as defined in section 5903 (5) sexual abuse of children as defined in section 6312 (6) sexual exploitation of children as defined in section 6320. GRADING: A violation of section (A) is (1) an offense of the same grade and degree as the most serious underlying offense in subsection (a) for which the defendant contacted the minor, or (2) a felony of the third degree, whichever is greater.

There were more charges. Counts 2-12 were the eleven photographs of the nude minor children projected by Smith over the Internet to school Brianna on the art of masturbation. Each of these counts were Felony-3 charges under 18 Pa.C.S. 6312(d)(1). Count 13 of the original prosecution was Criminal Use of a Communication Facility, i.e. using his computer webcam to commit a crime (masturbating for Agent Brianna Osinski). This was another Felony3 under 18 Pa.C.S. 7512(a). The thirteen Felony-3 counts could parlay into a ninety-one-year prison term, plus fines and court costs. Normally, a felony would also include restitution to the victim, but in this case, who was the victim?[16] All of these offenses had an "OFFENSE GRAVITY SCORE" of five, on a scale of one to fourteen. They were equivalent in gravity to committing thirteen simultaneous offenses such as possession with intent to deliver one to ten pounds of marijuana, theft of $2000 to $25000, second time DUI offender 13X, or burglary of a structure that no one lives in thirteen times over.

The guidelines for one such offense were RS (Restorative Sanctions) to nine months, plus or minus three months; in other words, zero to twelve months minimum sentence (assuming the defendant had no prior record). The much-revered sentencing guidelines in this case provide little helpful guidance to involved parties, as a standard range for the thirteen offenses would be zero days to thirteen years!

The search warrant allowing seizure of the Sergeant's computer yielded some additional felony charges. These charges were under subsection 4, obscenity. (As part of

---

16 The only victims in the case were the poor girls whose photos Osinski passed around in the case. These were real naked people he showed Smith and whoever else became involved in the case.

pre-trial discovery, I was provided copies of the infants who were photographed nude. Although they were clearly young women/girls, none of them were pre-pubescent. All were mature and some had fashioned substantial mammillary accessories. It would seem that this should differentiate Mr. Smith from the sick-pup child pornographer who would photograph five-year-old children conducting sodomy with zebras, but under our law there is no difference.) And there were four more counts here. Counts 5-8 under the new charges were unlawful use of communication facility based on the same obscene material. Eight more felonies were charged, with seven years maximum each and OFFENSE GRAVITY SCORE of five. The tally was now up to 147 years maximum.

What is a defense lawyer to do? There is no defense to these charges other than technical challenges to the computer storage and retrieval machinations. Once the client admits that he has disseminated the masturbating materials, there is little chance that such a challenge would be worthwhile. And if the challenge failed, the Defendant would be forced to pay the Commonwealth computer expert witness fees. Assuming the computer evidence lined up, it is inconceivable that a defendant would be acquitted in Western Pennsylvania, given the reading of the law as set forth above. The sympathy for child pornographers is on a level of the sympathy that one would receive defending Osama Bin Laden or Bernie Madoff.

Another deterrent for me going all the way to a trial in these cases was the Deputy Attorney General in charge of the prosecution. It depended upon the day, but I believe in general he gave me the creeps more so than the defendant. There is no way I would have allowed this A.G. to give my fourteen-year-old daughter a ride to cheerleading practice, even if I was five under par out on the twelfth hole of the golf course when the time came for transportation.

He was far too interested in the photographs. In fact, if it was between Mr. Smith and the Attorney General giving my daughter the ride to practice (if I had birdied no. 13, hypothetically) I would have given Smith the nod, albeit reluctantly.

At the plea hearing, we were only able to have three of the charges dropped, leaving nineteen Felony counts. Under the guidelines, it was inconceivable that Mr. Smith would escape further prison time, and he did not.

The Judge sentenced him on June 8, 2008 to a cumulative term of eighteen to thirty-six months prison (State Penitentiary) followed by six years probation. At a sentence modification hearing on August 26, 2008, his sex counselor provided compelling testimony that under the current prison regulations, he would not be out of prison for several years beyond the minimum due to the backup and length of the in-house sexual offender programs. She also testified that Smith was responding favorably to her own treatment outside the jail setting. The Deputy Attorney General opposed the motion on principal but had no evidence or argument other than the "seriousness of the charges" and the fact that the sentences were "within the standard guideline ranges."

On November 20, 2008, the Judge ruled. He reduced Smith's sentence to twelve months to twenty-four months, followed by six years probation. This was significant in that Mr. Smith could now serve the balance of his term in the county yard versus the state system. He could continue his current treatment regime with his current counselor and even be released for work. He may be able to keep his house. It was a major upgrade from his sentence on June 8.

But nothing was going right for Joe Smith. The Judge failed to issue the appropriate transport order. There was a breakdown in the process and no order was ever entered by the sentencing judge to move him back to Lawrence

County. Letters and calls to the Judge's chambers were ineffectual. Smith served two months beyond his minimum at the state facility in Camp Hill, PA, and began writing letters to everyone. And after several apologies as to how Mr. Smith was lost in the system, the case died.

There are three points to Mr. Smith's case. The first is based upon the crimes actually charged and how they were set up. Do we really have the resources, and if so, do we really want to spend these resources to entrap Internet masturbators with child porn and put them in prisons? Do special criminal statutes carved out by politicians yearning to look like heroes, which eradicate time-honored defenses to crimes, warp the playing field? Second, do the sentencing guidelines serve any real purpose in most cases? And third, how many people are really lost in the Great American Prison system, despite the best efforts of their counsel and others to get them proper legal attention? All three issues right now are weighed heavily in favor of the government. We must look at the costs and effectiveness of such policies and examine them with respect to their erosion of personal privacy, liberty, and sovereignty. Have the politicians helped us cross over a line to create Yardbird USA?

# CHAPTER 11

# The Flabby Crimes Code

Yes, the sun seemed to shine brighter then and the winter nights did not seem so bleak. It is tempting to wax sentimental if you are a student of common sense and wisdom. Under the old common law, defining crime and punishment was simple and effective. Starting with the basics of grading criminal offenses, this banal task did not require explanation from a third-year law professor at Columbia University, but now I suggest the professor, no matter how scholarly, would flounder at times.

Think of a single die with six spots. Roll a one and it's a Felony of the first degree. Roll a two and it's a Felony of the second degree. Roll a three and it's a Felony of the third degree. Roll four and it's a Misdemeanor of the first degree, and five and six are second and third degree Misdemeanors. Maximum jail terms and fines are established for each classification and the judge imposes the penalty face to face and directly upon the defendant based upon his judgment of the severity of the injury to the victim, the defendant's prior record with the law, and his/her remorse or lack thereof.

Such a simple and effective system could never go without demolition by do-good politicos. Now, instead of a dice, we have a six deck, or "shoe" of cards, and this six deck "shoe" has been shuffled like a blackjack deck on a shuffling machine at the Golden Nugget Casino. We have hundreds of offenses classified not only by statutory class but also under "offense gravity scores" and "prior record points." Under the Pennsylvania Code, I counted over 750 separate criminal classifications consuming twenty-five pages of text. By the time this chapter is finished, there will likely be additional criminal offenses invented by the legislature, and/or existing offenses will be further subdivided and parsed. Each such effort pins down a sentencing court more and more and eliminates discretion and judgment from the process. Each new offense criminalizes more behavior and each classification guideline pigeonholes such conduct into cookie cutter outcomes—usually being more jail time to satisfy the hunger of crime tough politicos.

In Pennsylvania, there are hundreds of crimes in the crimes code, many of them totally unnecessary. For example, as if the catchall crime of "Disorderly Conduct" (18 Pa.C.S.A. 4403) is not broad enough to encompass about anything offensive to a police officer, we also have "Disrupting Meetings" (18 Pa.C.S.A. 5508), "Unauthorized School Bus Entry" (18 Pa.C.S.A. 5517), Fortune Telling (18 Pa.C.S.A. 7104), Furnishing Free Insurance (18 Pa.C.S.A. 7310)[17], and Deception Relating to Kosher Foods (18 Pa.C.S.A. 4107.1). Furnishing Drug-Free Urine is now a specially coded crime [18 Pa.C.S.A. 7509(a)], as is Unlawful Sale of Term Papers [18 Pa.C.S.A. 7324].

Apparently, criminalizing conduct offensive to humanity not righteous enough in this nation of state intermeddling. We are now criminalizing conduct that is offensive to animals. We may soon reach the point where road killing a possum or teasing a pet bunny rabbit results in a jail term.

---

17 Any guess as to whether the sponsor of this act may have some connection to the insurance lobby?

On November 6, 2011 Nicholas J. Wooddell of Beaver County, Pennsylvania punched his grammy's dog. Apparently, this was a crisis that could not be handled by the family internally, so Wooddell was charged with multiple criminal offenses and placed in jail until he could make bond.* These days, no situation is beyond the reach of the criminal justice system in Yardbird USA.

When we move from the crimes code to other chapters of Pennsylvania Statutes, the codification of criminal conduct becomes even more absurd. There are crimes under the Vehicle Code, the Clean Streams Act, the Controlled Substances Devices and Cosmetics Act, the Chop Shop Act, the Solid Waste Disposal Act, the Domestic Relations Act, the Education Code, the Welfare Code, the Fish and Game Acts—on, on, and on. I have practiced law for a quarter century and could find a new criminal offense every day if necessary. In the game law, offenses are classified from Misdemeanor One (M-1) Offenses through Misdemeanor Three (M-3) offenses, and then Summary Offenses from eighth degree down to first degree! [34 Pa.C.S.A. 925(b)]. In the Game law the legislature felt compelled to enact definitions of obtuse and incomprehensible terms such as: "person," "arrow," "bird," and "time."

"Time" is defined in the code as "Official prevailing time," believe it or not, and an "arrow" is "a missile shot from a bow, having a slender shaft with fletching or vanes at the butt and a pointed head without any explosive, chemical or poison in the head or shaft and used solely with a bow" (34 Pa.C.S.A. 102). Such invaluable definitional mandates will surely relieve the courts from burdensome debates over what "time" it was when a dropping fell from a "bird."

---

* Police: Man Punched Dog, Temesonline.com:Local News Nov. 6, 2011; PA Docket Number: MJ-36304-CR-0000181-2011]

The legislatures are not bashful about choosing favorites either. If you work for the government and you are a crime victim, the offender is punished at a higher level, as opposed to a private person victim, at least when it comes to an assault. Assaulting your insurance agent, your doctor, your lawyer, your nurse, your pastor, or your mom is a felony of the second degree. However, under the exact same facts, if your mom is a police officer, firefighter, probation officer, sheriff, deputy sheriff, liquor control agent, jail guard, judge, district attorney or assistant district attorney, public defender or assistant public defender, any person in federal state or local law enforcement, parking officer, constable, teacher, governor, auditor general, state treasurer, member of the General Assembly, or any number of such other government or quasi-government official (thirty-six to be exact), then you have not a second degree felony but a first degree felony [18 Pa. C.S.A. 2702(c)]. The difference can be up to ten years more in the penitentiary. Is the government trying to tell us that theirs are more important victims than common private individuals?

While pawing through my Criminal Justice Manual one evening, I located the gem of all gems: a block of gold with a faultless diamond shining on top. The treasure I found is the perfect illustration of both points made above: (1) the officious intermeddling by politicians in the legal system, carving out stupendously imaginative offenses with one hand, and (2) the protection and elevation of the public sector parasite to darling status with the other.

Assume that you are driving down a country road in the summertime, sipping on an ice-cold Coca Cola and enjoying the open air of the season. You come upon a construction site where the highway department is patching one lane's potholes and you are directed to stop by a middle-aged cretin of a man. You stop your vehicle as opposing traffic passes, but you are not directed to proceed as several minutes go by. The sign-holding cretin approaches you and says he is very hot and thirsty and will let you pass through if you give him the rest of your Coke plus ten dollars. Reluctantly and seeing little choice, you hand the cretin ten dollars and the remainder of your Coke, and he lets you through at last. When you get to the sign-holder on the opposite end of the construction site, you ask for the name of the cretin who took your money and Coke. Being of below-average intellect, the sign holder complies and you contact the state police, who have jurisdiction over any irregularities in or about the construction site.

Now read Section 2293 of the PA Highways and Bridges Act: "If any person working upon any road or highway, or if anyone in company with such person, shall ask money or reward, or by any means whatsoever, shall extort or endeavor to extort, any money, drink, or other thing, of or from any person traveling upon or near such road or highway, the person so offending shall, for every such offense, forfeit and pay a sum not exceeding five dollars" (36 P.S. 2293).

It is clear that for such legislation to have actually been enacted a state legislator's young son must have been talked out of his Coke plus $10, leading to the conception of this extraordinary, unspeakable crime. But before the ink was dry on this legislation, it must have been discovered that the flag-holding cretin who committed the offense was the paramour of another legislator, thus ensuring that the fine would be less than the booty collected at the gate. The public worker, even if hammered with the maximum fine of $5 by the Judge, still comes out with quenched thirst and $5 in his pocket as a result of the shakedown.

Back in the day of raison d'être and common sense, the criminal law consisted of a few common law crimes that covered any conceivable illegal, criminal activity in which another person was harmed: burglary, larceny, assault, battery, forgery, arson, homicide, rape, and a few others. There was no crimes code but merely case law, which assimilated decades of cases into a predictable and reasonable regimen.

All of that has changed, as we have seen. The frenetic desire to codify criminal law and include any offensive conduct as a crime, so that politicians can look good, has led to a proliferation of criminal statutes, rules, and procedures. My 2010 Criminal Justice Handbook, which merely identifies all crimes and offenses in Pennsylvania, plus the Rules of Criminal Procedure (i.e., no annotations or comments at all) contains 350 pages. *And this is just the index.* The text itself is another 1,772 pages, making this fat, sloppy book a total of 2,122 pages. The Holy Bible I was presented when I first joined my church contained only 981 pages.

The NFL Super Bowl Trophy is named after the great Vince Lombardi, legendary coach of the Green Bay Packer football dynasty. Lombardi, despite his autocratic reputation, was not much for rules. He told his terrified new team at the start of the 1969 season that he will have "as few rules as he can get away with."* Self motivation, self discipline, and pride propelled Lombardi and his teams to success, not a constant fear of violating rules and regulations of the coach. In Yardbird USA, we are taking the opposite path of Coach Lombardi. Our government is whipping up layer after layer of bureaucratic regulations and penalties upon us. This is the game plan of losers.

---

* "When Pride Still Mattered: A Life of Vince Lombardi", Maraniss, David, p. 468

# CHAPTER 12

# Timothy Zimburger
# and The Abuse of Bail

Tim Zimburger was a regular American, a forty-five-year-old Union Worker from northwestern Pennsylvania who stood only five feet, five inches tall and weighed but 150 pounds. Facing off against the American Legal Juggernaut, he was helpless as a sick lamb.

Though it was not the stuff of the American Dream, Tim was, alas, living the protocol of the common American Family: Two stepdaughters—Lacey and her younger sister, and a natural son made by union with his current wife. The marriage was a struggle, pressured by financial concerns as work was scarce for Tim during the recession of 2007-2010. Tim's wife was a substance abuser and contributed little to the family package. Somehow the stepdaughter, now fifteen years old, was an honor student in high school. Lacey had no contact whatsoever with her natural father, who lived in Ohio. Although she had had regular contact with him for several years, something had occurred recently that caused Lacey to shun him and she would not speak to him at the 2007 summer family reunion.

_Commonwealth v. S J Z_ (No. 458 Crim. 2009 Mercer County)

Lacey showed up at Children and Youth Services on November 17, 2008 at 6:30 p.m. Her mother had placed a phone call to the agency earlier that day and Mom was advised to bring Lacey in to talk. Lacey gave a statement to CYS investigators with her mother present in the room. Lacey gave the following statement, according to Pennsylvania State Police: The sexual abuse began when she was age six or seven. Lacey advised that the first instance of abuse that she could recall occurred when she and her mother and sister were living with her stepfather in a trailer in Sandy Lake, Pennsylvania. She advised that it was around Christmas time and that she was lying on the couch of the residence watching television and that the abuser came into the residence and that her mother was not with him. She advised that the abuser sat on the couch next to her and that she was covered up with a blanket. Lacey said that the abuser reached under the blanket and removed her pants and underwear, and that she asked him what he was doing, and that he advised her that she would like what he was going to do. Lacey said that he then put his head under the blanket and performed oral sex on her. She advised that approximately one month later she was again in the living room and that the abuser came into the room and asked her to give him a massage. She advised that the abuser removed all of his clothing and had her rub his back for about ten minutes. Lacey then stated that the abuser turned over so he was lying on his back and that he had her rub his penis. She advised that he told her that she could not stop until he told her that she could. Lacey advised that eventually a whitish, clear fluid came out of his penis and that he then told her that she could stop. Lacey remembered that there were several occa-sions where the abuser would ask her to give him a massage or he would make her wrestle him while they were both naked. Lacey was asked how often these kinds of things would go on and she stated that it occurred about once or twice a month. She also advised that there were times when the abuser would get into the bath tub with her and that he would touch her private area and that he would make her touch his penis. Lacey advised that part of the way through her first grade year the family moved to the Hadley, Pennsylvania, area (northern part of the county of Mercer). She further advised that the sexual abuse continued by the same abuser. She states that she recalled another instance of oral sex that occurred while the family was living in Hadley. She further states that the last contact of a sexual nature occurred at the residence in Hadley and during this instance the abuser assaulted her by inserting a "Harry Potter" wand in her vagina. Lacey stated that he moved the wand back and forth in her vagina and her sister witnessed the incident and even asked what the abuser was doing, whereupon the abuser said, "Lacey would like it and do not say anything." Lacey was asked why she had never reported this before. She claimed that her stepfather had threatened to "throw her through a wall" if she told her mother, and that she was often hit in the head, face, and stomach by the abuser. Lacey also stated that the abuser would attempt to get her and her younger sister to wrestle each other naked, or that he would ask her to play a game and told her that if she lost she would have to do what he said and that he would want her to give him a back rub or wrestle him naked.

It would not take much imagination to figure out who the abuser was: Right, Tim Zimburger, the stepfather, the textbook suspect in child abuse legend and lore. The State Trooper who investigated the charges interviewed the mother/wife and she stated she knew nothing about the abuse. The Trooper then interviewed Mr. Zimburger, who emphatically denied the allegations. The Trooper then attempted to interview the sister, who was an alleged eyewitness. It was noteworthy to me that the Trooper never did interview the sister because the mother "spoke to her and she (Lacey) did not remember anything" and this was enough for the Trooper; no interview occurred. I give the

Trooper credit in that he did not file the charges based on what he heard, which was an uncorroborated allegation of sexual abuse, but rather passed the ball to the District Attorney's office. An assistant District Attorney advised him to file the "appropriate charges" against the defendant.

The Arrest Warrant, dated March 27, 2009, alleged charges of Rape, Rape of a Child, Involuntary Deviate Sexual Intercourse (two counts), Statutory Sexual Assault, Aggravated Indecent Assault (two counts), Indecent Assault (two counts), Harassment. The mandatory sentences would cumulate twenty years and if all offenses ran consecutively the total would be over one hundred years' imprisonment. All Criminal Conduct was alleged to have occurred between 1999 and 2003, six to ten years ago! And these sick and horrendous acts were never reported until March of 2009.

The District Judge who set the bail for Mr. Zimburger had only one comment: these are very serious charges. A bail of $100,000 was set. Mr. Zimburger was unable to post bond and was placed in the Mercer County Prison. To post bail in this amount a defendant would have to come up with that amount in cash ($100,000) or hire a bail bondsman, who would require a bail bond premium in the amount of 7 percent of the bail ($7,000), which is non-refundable. This bond acts as security for the appearance of the defendant, and if the defendant were to abscond, the bail agency would be required to either cough up the $100,000 (very rare) or send out its "goon squad" to locate the defendant. In very high bail cases, the bail bondsman will obtain virtually all personal information available, from scars and tattoos to family members out of town, to bank accounts, vehicle information, etc., that would assist in tracking down the defendant. But a defendant with genuine ties to the community (such as close family) is rarely a flight risk, no matter how serious the charges are. Almost all absconders from criminal charges are transients.

This bail was so far off the charts that it was almost mind-blowing. Zimburger had no significant prior criminal record, a job and family in the local area, and was no flight risk whatsoever. He had custody of his five-year-old son! Bail is meant to secure the appearance of the accused for his or her court appearances. To a lesser degree, it is meant to assure protection of the alleged victim and family. But the case had already been turned over to Children and Youth Services and the child (now nearly sixteen years old) was under their protective bureaucracy. There were not even any allegations of criminal sexual abuse since 2003. But now the government demands a bail of $100,000 to rest assured of Mr. Zimburger's appearances in court!

Zimburger was placed in jail on March 27, 2009, in lieu of $100,000 bail where he sat with no legal attention until his preliminary hearing on April 4.

Mr. Zimburger was represented by the Public Defender and waived his Preliminary Hearing (first mistake) with the understanding that he would take a polygraph (second mistake). An additional felony one (F-1) charge was added. (After I became convinced of Mr. Zimburger's innocence, I discussed a polygraph with the District Attorney. Although I totally distrust the polygraph procedure, it can be a win-win for an accused. If he passes the polygraph, the charges are dismissed. If he fails, the fact that a polygraph was even administered is not admissible in court, so no member of the jury would even know about it. One condition I requested pursuant to the polygraph was that no statements made by Mr. Zimburger during the polygraph could be used in evidence at trial. I required this condition because Mr. Zimburger had already given a statement to the police denying the charges. But there is no way for him to duplicate this denial word for word and thus his statements in the polygraph examination would be "inconsistent" or "contradictory." The District Attorney would not agree to this, so I refused the polygraph offer. This made it clear that the government's motive was not to exonerate a potentially innocent man but to gather evidence against him.)

No bail reduction was requested. In the meantime Mr. Zimburger was to sit in the county jail and wallow in his own feces, a man presumed innocent at this point in time.

His family contacted me on April 6, 2009, and I visited Mr. Zimburger in the County Jail a few days later. I prepared a bond reduction petition and entered my appearance for Mr. Zimburger on May 7, 2010. The Judge heard testimony from his family members. The Judge heard that he was deeply rooted in Mercer County, Pennsylvania, having lived all his life in the area. Mr. Zimburger supported himself, being employed through a carpenter's union and entering his busy season. The Judge heard evidence that he had siblings and a mother living in western Pennsylvania and that he resided with his only son, Tim, Jr., who was five years old. No one in their right mind would consider him a flight risk, and that is the main consideration in setting bail, as stated previously. Secondary considerations are protection of the alleged victim and the strength of the pending case against him. The Judge wants to avoid retaliatory situations, threats to witnesses, and allowing a potential danger into the community. However, the last alleged incident here was in 2003. The alleged victim was now sixteen years old. There were no other pending charges, nor any allegations that Mr. Zimburger had molested anyone else. No physical evidence supported the charges against him, only the bald allegations of his step-daughter Lacey.

The District Attorney opposed the bail reduction and the basis was that the allegations set forth by Lacey were "not the type of allegations that could be fabricated." The specificity and weirdness of the claims apparently sancti-fied them with credibility. In other words, no one could make up the wrestling scenarios and the Harry Potter wand story. The Judge permitted the District Attorney to read the affidavit of probable cause, which outlined the claim of Lacey. Although he is not to decide the case at a bail reduction hearing, the Judge clearly is impacted by the nature of the bald accusations. It is a mistake to get into the allegations of the case because the defense is not about to put on a case, even if he were prepared to do so at this stage in the proceedings. The victim is not there for cross-examination. Finally, it makes no real difference how strong the Commonwealth's case is at this point; the determination of guilt or innocence can only be made at trial.

The Judge imposed some conditions on bail. First, there could be no contact with the complainant (Lacey) or her immediate family. Second, Mr. Zimburger could have no contact with any person under the age of eighteen. The first condition was acceptable and in fact desirable. The second condition was nothing short of ridiculous. But he could live with it. It meant that his brother and sister-in-law would have to care for his five-year-old son. The bail itself was lowered from $100,000 to $50,000 cash or surety. This meant that Mr. Zimburger would have to post $50,000 cash (refundable at the end of the case) or post a surety bond with a bail bondsman. This would require payment of a non-refundable premium of the standard 7 percent, or $3,500. In the midst of an economic meltdown in a weak economic area, this was a substantial amount.

Let's step back and look at the absurdity of this scenario. If the defendant has access to money, he can post either the $100,000 or the $50,000 bail. The only difference is how much we feather the nest of the bail bonding agency. The bail bonding agency makes easy money because the defendant is going absolutely nowhere. The Judge protects the alleged victim with the other portions of the bail order prohibiting any contact. This would apply whether the bail was $5,000 or $50,000. Once bail is posted, it is only this condition that "protects" the alleged victim, regardless of the amount of the bail itself.

At this stage in the case the Defendant is presumed innocent, yet he must yield to these conditions and pay $3,500 for his pre-trial release. Most Defendants in this situation could not afford to post bail of $50,000 in Mercer County, Pennsylvania. Most defendants would occupy a cell in the county calaboose until his or her case came to issue. Many defendants are guilty as charged and end up serving time and their time spent in jail pending resolution of their case counts toward their ultimate sentence. But many defendants are not guilty as charged and many more, if not most, end up pleading guilty to lesser charges. Some defendants actually take plea bargains to lesser charges on weak cases since they already have substantial time served, and by the time they are sentenced, their release is imminent. In this situation we have everything backwards. The sentence is served upon arrest, the plea bargain is heavily influenced by the defendant's position in jail, and then the defendant gets out at sentence court, having served his term and then some already.

Back to Mr. Zimburger's case. Fortunately for Zimburger, his family came up with the money to bail him out on May 7, 2009. He had been totally confined in jail for a total of six weeks.

It is a tremendous disadvantage for a defendant to sit in jail while the government sets the stage for his trial. Imagine if complainants, police, and other government witnesses were locked up until the case went to trial. Yet many defendants are. By definition, they already have limited resources, or they would bail themselves out. I know that the conviction rate for my clients who have sat behind bars while trial preparation occurred is much higher than the conviction rates for defendants out on bail and assisting with their defense, and I believe this is the general rule across the country. The playing field is leveled somewhat when a defendant secures his or her pre-trial release. And it is no wonder that prosecutors object to bail reductions and the release of defendants before trial.

When Mr. Zimburger was released, it gave us an opportunity to take our time and research his defense. We had an investigator look into the family history. We obtained records from Children and Youth Agency. We talked to dozens of potential witnesses, including neighbors, mutual friends, and baby sitters. We looked at Lacey's school records. We looked at the mother. The mother was a substance abuser with various arrests and was on parole for Driving Under the Influence. There were indications of bipolar disorder. Although I never got the opportunity to cross-examine her, the image I received of her was that of a woman who had been ridden hard and put away wet.

We issued subpoenas to several witnesses who saw Lacey interact with Tim on a normal basis. People close to Lacey would testify that she would have confided in them if there were an abusive situation. Mom had some DUI charges and was facing a probation violation. Rumors were that she wanted to leave the state. Character witnesses were lined up to show that the alleged conduct by Mr. Zimburger would be so far out of character to be laughable. Reports that Lacey's natural father in Ohio was the one who broke the ties with Lacey proved to be bogus and reversed. It was clear that Lacey inexplicably cut the ties with him at a family reunion, which was strange because Lacey's younger sister remained in close contact with the natural father.

But as in any case of sexual abuse, we faced the confounding question of why would Lacey make up such a story? Where would she come up with these scenarios? Why would she come forward if it were not true? In other words, what was her motive to lie?

In preparing for the trial, I had developed sort of a "spreadsheet" of the activities of Mom and Lacey from August 2008 to the time of the arrest in March of 2009.

This required us to weave in the happenings with the Children and Youth Services, the Domestic File in Mercer and Crawford County, and the police reports.

Here is how this scenario played out. It becomes evident that the scenario is both bizarre and yet predictable.

**December 2007.** Tim Zimburger and wife/mom separate. Mom kicked out for drunkenness and infidelity. Lacey holds grudge against Tim.

**August 29, 2008.** Mom files for custody of five-year-old son.

**October 28, 2008.** Mom loses custody of son at mediation, due in part to her alcohol problems.

**November 17, 2008.** Mother makes phone call to Children and Youth Services reporting sexual abuse of Lacey and requesting appointment for Lacey to discuss matter. Mom and Lacey go in for interview and mom stays with Lacey throughout.

**November 19, 2008.** Children and Youth "Safety Plan" developed, which includes no contact with "AP" (alleged perpetrator). Mom admits marijuana use and being an alcoholic.

**March 27, 2009.** Police arrest Timothy Zimburger for alleged sexual abuse of Mom's daughter Lacey.

**March 27, 2009.** Mom files Modification of Custody and Divorce Papers vs. Tim Zimburger, her husband.

**April 27, 2009.** Mr. Zimburger competes with mom for custody of five-year-old son in Mediation Conference. Mom is in the courthouse and Mr. Zimburger participates by phone from jail.

**May 6, 2009.** Mom awarded sole legal and primary physical custody of five-year-old son. Tim to have no physical contact with the child and only one phone call per day.

During the summer and fall we continued our investigation in the case. Lacey's mother continued to meander along in and out of substance abuse programs, keeping Timothy's five-year-old son from him except during the times she wanted to go out and get drunk. This occurred over the Fourth of July weekend, among others. The alleged child rapist was a convenient place for her to drop off her five–year-old son while she partied. Apparently the fear that the child would be penetrated by some type of firework device was not considered by Mom, or if it was considered, she must have felt the risk was outweighed by her desire to achieve intoxication.

During the fall the case was continued as we waited for Mom to completely implode. But the time had come where this case had to be resolved, as the pending case was impairing Mr. Zimburger's work opportunities and preventing him from normal relations with his child. We were ready for trial in January 2010. Somewhat unexpectedly, the Commonwealth moved for a continuance in January "so that the Commonwealth can obtain information from the victim's school records and otherwise prepare for trial." This continuance was granted over our objection.

One of the interesting aspects of this type of criminal case is the admission into evidence of the recorded interview of the "victim," typically given to a caseworker. The normal scenario is for the victim to testify at trial, then be cross-examined by the defense lawyer, at which time her credibility is attacked. The Commonwealth is then typically permitted to introduce the tape of the interview with the caseworker to show "prior consistent statements" made by the victim to bolster her credibility. Defense attorneys have argued that such testimony should not be admitted, as it was given under circumstances that do not permit cross-examination by counsel. In other words, it violates the "confrontation clause" of the constitution. The Commonwealth gets the testimony in under a hearsay exception of prior consistent statements with a caveat that such statements are not admitted "for their truth or veracity but only to show that prior consistent statements were made at another time." I, and other defense lawyers, believe that such cautionary instructions are like spraying Lysol on road kill. In a trial I had several months previous to this case in Mercer County, the Judge allowed the videotape of the "victim's" statement to come into evidence. I was allowed to argue that the jury had no idea what the examiner said to the "victim" prior to the interview. I was able to point out that I was not invited to ask any questions at that time. And most importantly, I was allowed to point out that the taped interview did not require the "victim" to be sworn in under oath to tell the truth. My client was acquitted of all charges in that case[18], but it is a very hopeless feeling to sit at the trial and watch a DVD recording where a very sympathetic and gullible caseworker is spoon-feeding leading questions to an alleged victim, with the jury anxiously listening and watching.

Lacey submitted to just such an interview, and I was able to watch it as part of pre-trial discovery. Lacey came off as a reserved, almost reluctant storyteller, but she stuck to her story and made a very good appearance for herself. Undoubtedly coached by the counselor as to how to handle the interview, Lacey gave no appearance that she was fabricating this weird story. Based upon Mom's time line (outlined above), I felt we had pretty concrete proof that Mom had put Lacey up to the whole thing to further her own interests. It was my intention not to cross-examine Lacey at all. Then the District Attorney would have no basis on which to play the set-up interview. This, of course, was a risk in and

---

18 *Commonwealth v. JRP*, CR No.1094-2008 Mercer County.

of itself, but again, we were confident that the extraordinary time period in which these alleged events were not reported, along with the time line chart, would blow the government's case out of the water. I was not about to let the jury see some pre-recorded interview that set my client up as the criminal.

We went to the pre-trial conference in February ready to go to trial that month, confident but realizing that Mr. Zimburger's fate was totally in the hands of twelve strangers.

We never seated a jury to decide the ultimate question of guilt or innocence. On the eve of trial at the pre-trial conference, and after several postponements of the trial, the District Attorney asked the Judge to *noll pros* (dismiss) the case. On February 2, 2010, nearly a year after his arrest and incarceration, the government dropped everything against Mr. Zimburger, with a whisper to the Judge at side bar. Mr. Zimburger was not even present to observe the case against him go flaccid and fall to a silent, ignominious death. A court order is entered nolle prossing the charges, almost in secret. Mr. Zimburger had been dirtied and stained by his forty-two days of incarceration in the Mercer County Prison for no reason. In that time period he lost rank at his union position and missed several job opportunities. He lost custody of his five-year-old son. He expended thousands of dollars in legal fees and bail bond premiums. He has been branded a child abuser in the Commonwealth of Pennsylvania, even though no criminal charges stuck. And he bears the blotch of a child abuse charge evidenced by a significant time voucher at the county prison.

# CHAPTER 13

# A New Look At Bail
# Under The Constitution

The United States Constitution's Eighth Amendment (and the Pennsylvania State Constitution under Article I, Section 13) states, in part, "Excessive Bail shall not be required." Interestingly it does not state who should be required to post (pay for) bail for a defendant. Since the Amendment purports to protect the rights of individuals versus the government, the argument can be made that the Amendment infers that the Defendant should not be subject to excessive bail. But let us look at the issue of bail from the opposite side of the fence. Why should the Commonwealth not have to post the bail? The Defendant is merely accused of a crime at the point of his arrest and by the Constitution he or she is presumed innocent until proven guilty beyond a reasonable doubt. Bail should be the obligation of the government. The government should have to pay the cost of insuring that an innocent person appears for trial unless the presumption of innocence is overcome.

Looking back at the history of Anglo Saxon law, freemen were not subject to imprisonment save for crimes against the crown or other heinous offenses. Nearly all crimes involved a penalty of fines. Bail was typically in the amount of the potential fine and was to secure the appearance of the freeman and payment of the fine if convicted.[19] With regard to fines, it was clear that a defendant had to post the bail to cover a potential conviction. But when penalties change from monetary fines, which are common as civil penalties in many situations, to total deprivation of liberty in the form of imprisonment, an entirely different scenario is created. In Anglo Saxon law, there was no such thing as pre-trial detention until the monetary system of penalty was replaced by corporal punishment. Bail conditions were set forth in the Statute of Westminster in 1275. Abuses suffered by defendants led the Quakers of Pennsylvania to adopt the Great Law of 1682, which made bail available to all offenders, including capital offenses unless the "proof was evident and the presumption great." This language has been adopted by many other states so Pennsylvania is certainly the rule rather than the exception.

This traditional right to freedom before conviction permits the unhampered preparation of a defense, and serves to prevent the infliction of punishment prior to conviction. Unless the right to bail before trial is preserved, the presumption of innocence, secured only after centuries of struggle, would lose its meaning [*Stack v. Boyle*, 342 U.S. 1 (1951)]. "The practice of admission to bail, as it has evolved in Anglo American law, is not a device for keeping persons in jail upon mere accusation until it is found convenient to give them a trial. On the contrary, the spirit of the procedure is to enable them to stay out of jail until a trial has found them guilty. Without this conditional privilege, even those wrongly accused are punished by a period of imprisonment while awaiting trial and are handicapped in consulting counsel, searching for evidence and witnesses,

---

19 June Carbone, Seeing Through the Emperor's Clothes: Rediscovery of Basic Principles in the Administration of Bail, *Syracuse L. Rev.* 517 (1983).

and preparing a defense (Ex Parte Milburn, 9 L.Ed. 280, at 7-8, the words of Justice Robert Jackson in 1835).

We can see from history that the original purpose of bail was not to exact money from accused defendants so that they could avoid incarceration. Abuses in bail requirements led us in Pennsylvania to demand that reasonable bail be available. The presumption of innocence is a joke if an accused sits in jail because he cannot post excessive bail. The idea of making a defendant come up with the money to post a bail set by a magisterial judge, with strong ties to the government and the bail bonding agencies, but generally weak ties to the constitution, contravenes the spirit of the Constitution. A magistrate who sets bail looks great in the paper when an accused child molester cannot post bail and is remanded to the county jail and he looks even better to a bail bondsman when the occasional defendant can come up with the money to post a bond. This insures that magistrates are invited to the extravagant balls and parties hosted by the bail bonding agencies that profit enormously from inflated bail bonds.

The party making the accusation against an accused defendant (the governmental agency) should be forced to post the monetary bond of an accused that is presumed innocent.

Let's look at every reasonable scenario. In all cases, the most equitable result is achieved if the government posts the bail.

Scenario No. 1. NOT GUILTY. Presently if a defendant, like Mr. Zimburger, posts bail, he pays a surety bondsman 7 percent (or thereabouts) for the bail piece. This is akin to an insurance premium that is not refunded. To obtain his pre-trial release the Defendant or his family must come up with this money. If he is acquitted or the charges are dropped, like Mr. Zimburger, the Defendant unjustly eats these costs. Under our theory of bail, the government has borne the cost of securing the Defendant's appearance, not the innocent defendant. This is clearly the more just result.

Scenario No. 2. GUILTY. The defendant appears for court and is convicted. The Commonwealth has posted the bail. The cost of the surety bond is added to the defendant's court costs to be paid along with other costs of the action. Presently, defendants are charged with all court costs, including the cost of subpoenas for their own witnesses, costs of government expert witnesses, laboratory fees for testing evidence, etc. Adding the cost of the bail bond is simply one more tangential cost of prosecution that needs to be recouped by the winning party—in this case the government.

Scenario No. 3. FUGITIVE. The defendant fails to appear. In this case the bonding company must attempt to secure the person of the Defendant or forfeit the amount of the bond to the government. There is virtually no difference in this scenario whether the bail is posted by the government or the defendant. There is another interesting point on the government posting bail rather than the defendant. It does not take a mental giant to figure out that the courts will naturally set lower bail for Defendants if the government will have to put up the money for the bail. Courts will not unnecessarily impose absurdly high bail amounts for no-risk defendants if the money comes from their state coffers rather than the defendant's family. Also, if there is a forfeiture, the courts will want to keep this amount as small as possible for the government whereas they could care less if the defendant had to put up the money to make bail.

Scenario No. 4. NO BAIL POSTED. An obviously guilty defendant who does not want to run up his or her court costs may elect to not post bail. He or she will stay in jail pre-trial and receive credit for time served.

Scenario No. 5. NO BAIL SET. Can the Bail Setting Authority simply deny any bail to the accused? If so, the Commonwealth would not have to put up any money for the Defendant's pre-trial release. This certainly could create gross abuses, but it would not be possible under the Constitution since only those crimes which carry a sentence of life imprisonment or death are "unbailable" offenses. All other offenses require reasonable bail to be set.

I invite anyone to set forth a scenario under the new look, requiring the government to post bail, which is impracticable and/or unfair. I don't believe it can be done. Clearly, jail overcrowding would be relieved substantially if the government posted bail for accused prisoners who had no money to do so on their own. More importantly, the presumption of innocence would be honored and individuals wrongly accused of a crime or individuals who successfully defend against charges of the government do not spend time behind bars.

The only downside to this "new look" at bail is for the inflated coffers of bail bonding agencies. Bail bond companies would be writing bonds for much lower premiums and would be in the unenviable position of having to rely on the government for its sustenance. Every dog has its day.

# CHAPTER 14

# Cody Williams Chooses Jail—The Debacle of Mandatory Sentencing

Cody Williams was born on November 9, 1982 and was a product of an apparently normal family environment. His parents maintained an intact marriage and supported Chris and his brother adequately as they grew up as normal Western Pennsylvania youth. The family had lived together in the Grove City area for over twelve years. Cody is a high school graduate. His father had developed a good business building water tanks. Cody's younger brother worked for the business and his mother handled the accounting.

Due to health problems, Cody was not able to work. Cody was diagnosed with Irritable Bowel Syndrome in 2005, at age twenty-three, and had been hospitalized with severe pain, dehydration, and vomiting at least ten times. He is prescribed five daily medications for this problem and is still symptomatic. He has lain on the table for a gall-bladder removal. He also has severe chronic back pain with multiple disc protrusions on MRI and focal areas of stenosis, causing pain and loss of mobility. Some of the evidence in the case suggested that Cody developed a dependency

---

*Commonwealth v. CRW* (No.339 Crim. 2007 Mercer County)

on painkillers. These ailments led Cody to successfully apply for disability benefits and he will likely not become a member of the shrinking American working class. Unfortunately, he would become a member of the growing class of prison yardbirds in our warped society.

Cody had been the victim of two minor assaults in recent history: a roughing up by Jason Kostelnik on December 1, 2004, and a pretty good pounding by Dusty Hoodley on December 20, 2006, both assaults being documented by court records. In June of 2006 he decided to purchase a gun.

Tommy Mayfair said he just wanted to be left alone. He was tired of Cody Williams "harassing him" by making cell phone calls to his fiancé and him. Tommy was a twenty-two-year-old boy who actually had never met Cody face to face.

Mayfair, originally from the Butler, PA, region, was wasting no time in developing a court record. A bounced check at Giant Eagle led to a civil case in 2004 that was later dropped when the bogus check was made good by someone on Mayfair's behalf. An assault charge against him in 2002 was reduced to Harassment and Mayfair pleaded guilty to that on May 6, 2003 at age eighteen. He was convicted of three speeding violations from 2004 to 2005 and another traffic offense in 2004. Mayfair committed another offense on January 13, 2007 when he showed up at the Williams residence without invitation or permission. He was never charged with a trespass because he was nearly killed as a result of the incident, and thus he became the "victim."

The person in dispute was a young lady named Barbie Hoffman. She was a twenty-seven-year-old white female residing in Grove City. Although she was technically Cody's "fiancée," this mother of two was apparently quite the flirt. Our investigation uncovered credible evidence that she was a cocaine addict and that she had developed considerable practice in the art of promiscuity. It was unlikely that Cody knew about either but he had to suspect both.

Barbie had seen Tommy and a couple of his buddies the night before at Wal-Mart, "cutting up," and somehow she hooked up with them the next day. Barbie arranged to have her daughter stay overnight at Alicia's house to visit Alicia's daughter. Barbie told Alicia that she would need a ride and Alicia showed up in a vehicle occupied by Tommy Mayfair and two young adults reeking of alcoholic beverages. Alicia was on probation. Cody's cell phone was working. The recipe for trouble was brewing.

Tommy apparently had a crush on Barbie, and Cody was in the way. According to Barbie's written statement, she heard comments uttered by Mayfair to the effect that he was ready to kick Cody's fat ass, knock him out, and on and on. Mayfair clearly wanted Williams' ass. Barbie stated that Tommy was talking aggressively the entire ride: "Let's take care of that fat ass Chris Wilson, and when I am done, they will not recognize his face."

On that cold, drab, winter night Mayfair took it upon himself to drive into the Grove City Hospital Parking Lot, directly across the street from the Williams residence. Despite being a strapping, muscular man standing about six-foot-two and carrying over two hundred pounds, he brought two friends with him as "witnesses." Cody, as we have described, was hardly an intimidating foe, however— a young man with a bovine build, suffering from crone's disease and a bad back—hardly capable of defending himself against an army of three.

To find the house Williams lived in, Mayfair and his two bodyguards enlisted the assistance of the girl that both boys were fighting over. Under her intelligent marshalling, the group proceeded to the north side of Grove City, parked at the hospital, and under cover of darkness, crossed Route 173 and walked up to the Williams residence.

Barbie stayed behind and stayed out of the game, indicating clearly that she was involved with both boys. The

**View of the Williams residence from parking lot of hospital**

next thing she heard was her friend Mandy yelling across the road, "Tommy's been shot!"

Inside, Cody's mom was making spaghetti and the NFL playoffs were on television. The New York Giants were upsetting the Dallas Cowboys on their way to the Super Bowl. It was a quiet evening for the Williams family at home, and even when the doorbell rang and a strange man stood in the doorway, Mrs. Williams did not suspect nor could she imagine what happened next. Mrs. Williams answered the door and saw Tommy Mayfair, whom she had never met, scowling at her on the porch. Mayfair asked for Cody, and Cody came to the door.

The exact sequence of events was never agreed upon and never will be, but it is clear that all three of the Mayfair clan walked onto the porch steps of the residence. It is clear that Cody faced three hostile hoods when he stepped outside. Mayfair immediately accused Cody of harassing him by cell phone and Cody demanded to know who he was.

Jack W. Cline

**Porch of Williams residence where assault and shooting occurred**

According to the Commonwealth witnesses, Cody "got in his face." It is undisputed that the first contact was made by the bozo, Mayfair. He pushed Cody down with such force that Cody tripped over one of the stairs and fell backwards onto the porch, defenseless. Just five feet away were Mayfair's beer muscled "witnesses."

Cody told me, and would testify at trial, that he was in fear for his life at this point in time. He was outnumbered at a ratio of 3:1 and he was outmatched by his primary foe, Tommy Mayfair, in size, strength, and agility. Cody actually feared that the situation could elevate into a home invasion and that his parents may be in danger. Cody's mother heard the commotion and opened the front door, screaming for the invaders to stop. Buffeted by the brief distraction, Cody gathered himself up and went into the house and retrieved a Ruger 89DC- 9mm double action hand gun.

Some of the observers believed that Cody had the gun on him all the time and others state he went back inside to fetch it out of a closet. Mayfair and his two witnesses, stupid to begin with plus plied with alcohol, stated that Cody never went back into the house. Williams stated that he pointed the gun at Mayfair and told him to get off the property. When Mayfair ignored the plea and charged Williams again, lurching for the gun, Cody fired a single shot and hit the Mayfair kid point blank. A bullet went through his abdomen, pierced an intestinal wall, and chipped a bone on the hip. Mayfair went down in excruciating pain and his two friends moved into action, displaying perhaps the only intelligent behavior that this scenario could offer. One of the thugs ran across the street to the hospital to see if the ambulance sitting there could drive over to the scene and provide transportation back to the hospital and perhaps administer critical emergency care to the immobilized Mayfair. But bureaucratic protocol prohibited the ambulance from leaving its parked position. Their only authorized response could be a proper dispatch from a 9-1-1 call. Fortunately, that is what the other thug did when he saw Mayfair go down in a heap.

Mayfair was taken by ambulance from Grove City Hospital to Allegheny General in Pittsburgh where he remained for eighteen days. He incurred over $75,000 in medical bills, much of them diagnostic. Several inches of his intestine were removed in surgery.

Cody Williams was charged with two counts of Aggravated Assault, a first-degree felony and a second-degree felony, along with related charges by the Pennsylvania State Police. The Information (charging document similar to an indictment) contained two lesser included simple assault counts, three counts of recklessly endangering another person, and two counts of terroristic threats for allegedly pointing the gun at Mayfair's backup trespassers on his porch. These terroristic threats counts, which appear almost as pile-on charges as Count 8 and 9, are actually

First Degree Misdemeanors carrying a maximum sentence of two and a half to five years.

If Cody was convicted of all counts in the Information, he was facing prison time of a maximum of twenty-five to fifty years. Fines could reach $95,000 plus costs and restitution to the victim's insurance carriers. Being that he had no prior criminal record, the chances of him receiving this severe a sentence was remote. However, the Judge will instruct the defendant that he could receive such a sentence prior to accepting a plea of guilty and a defense attorney must tell his client that this is the "exposure" he faces based upon the charges against him.

Most importantly, however, the Felony-1 aggravated assault case carried with it a minimum sentence of five years in a state penitentiary [42 Pa. C.S. A. Section 9712.1 (a)]. This mandatory sentence applies any time a firearm is involved in the offense[20]. This is a sentence of total confinement, with no chance of parole, work release, or furlough.

The legislature made it very clear that the Sentencing Court would be totally stripped of any authority to impose a sentence that would deviate downward from the legislative mandate, or that would apply any common sense to the circumstances at hand. Here is what the legislature in the Commonwealth of Pennsylvania spoketh: "(d) authority of court in sentencing. There shall be no authority in any court to impose on an offender to which this section is applicable any lesser sentence than provided for in subsection (a) or to place such offender on probation or to suspend sentence. Nothing in this section shall prevent the sentencing court from imposing a sentence greater than that provided in this section. Sentencing Guidelines promulgated by the Penn-

---

20 A firearm or replica of a firearm, reads the statute. Thus an air soft gun or even a high tech squirt gun could satisfy the requirements of this provision of Pennsylvania law.

sylvania Commission on Sentencing shall not supersede the mandatory sentences provided in this section."

Does this appear to be a coup by the legislature over the judiciary's authority to handle matters presented in its own courtroom? Is it an assault on the separation of powers? Has the legislature crossed over its boundary line?

Our defense in this case was, of course, justification. Justification is more commonly known as self-defense; however, it includes the claim of "defense of others." I became an expert in this defense years ago when I defended a young man who used a crochet mallet to ward off the attack of one of his peers (who happened to be the son of a State Police Corporal) on a defenseless young lady. The original charge of attempted homicide was presented admirably by a young District Attorney's assistant, but halfway through the trial, the judge would have no more. He called us into chambers and instructed us that the aggravated assault case would not be submitted to the jury and there should be a plea to simple assault. Normally in Mercer County, Pennsylvania, there would be no sentence bargain and the term of the sentence would not even be discussed with the trial judge, unless mandatory sentences were involved. But here, the Judge stated three months in the county jail was all the time my client was looking at for whacking the pate of a cocky Trooper's son who had himself become too physical with a girl. We took this deal and for months and months I would regret it because the defendant's mom called the office on a repetitive basis stating that he was a good kid and should not be in jail. There were demands to call the Bar Association, Disciplinary Board, and Fee Dispute Resolution Crisis Center, or whatever bureaucracy handled those issues at the time. At last, he got out and went to his doctor for some help.

Justification is a potent defense in Pennsylvania because the Commonwealth must disprove self-defense beyond a reasonable doubt in order to win a conviction. The down-side to that is that it is up to the trial judge whether or not self-defense can be presented to the jury for consideration.

Here is how the statute reads in Pennsylvania, and most other jurisdictions patterned after the Model Penal Code: "The use of force upon or towards another person is justifi-able when the actor believes that such force is immediately necessary for the purpose of protecting himself against the use of unlawful force by such other person on the present occasion" [18 Pa.CSA section 505(a)]. The statute goes on to state: "The use of deadly force is not justifiable under this section unless the actor believes that such force is necessary to protect himself against death, serious bodily injury, kidnapping or sexual intercourse compelled by threat or force; nor is it justifiable if; (i) the actor, with the intent of causing death or serious bodily injury, provoked the use of force against himself in the same encounter; or (ii) the actor knows that he can avoid the necessity of using such force with complete safety by retreating or by surren-dering possession of a thing to a person asserting a claim of right thereto or by complying with a demand that he abstain from any action which he has no duty to take, except that: (A) the actor is not obligated to retreat from his dwelling or place of work, unless he was the initial aggressor or is assailed in his place of work by another person whose place of work the actor knows it to be; and (B) a public officer justified in using force in the performance of his duties or a person justified in using force in his assistance or a person justified in using force in making an arrest or preventing an escape is not obligated to desist from efforts to perform such duty, effect such arrest or prevent such escape because of resistance or threatened resistance by or on behalf of the person against whom such action is directed. (iii) Except as required by paragraphs (1) and (2) of this subsection, a person employing protective force may estimate the necessity thereof under the circumstances as he believes them to be when the force is used, without retreating, surrendering possession, doing any other act which he has no legal duty to do or abstaining from any lawful action [18 Pa.CSA section 505(b)].

That's enough to give a law professor a headache, but that's the law, and only part of it. As applied to this case, in which Cody Williams used deadly force allegedly in self-defense against the attack by Billy Mayfair at the Williams residence, the law can be boiled down as follows: non-deadly force would have been appropriate under any circumstances but deadly force was used. The use of deadly force for self-protection is a subjective test based upon the circumstances believed to exist by the defendant at the time and place he is confronted with force. There is no duty to retreat in the home of the defendant. The defendant must be in fear of death or serious bodily injury to employ a deadly weapon.

The result of the self-defense assertion would depend upon the credibility of the witnesses, which is often the case in a criminal trial. Fortunately the family had the means to hire a private investigator to assist me in preparing for the trial. We use Ross-Graham, the principal being retired State Trooper Richard Graham, of Franklin, PA. Mr. Graham is thorough, insightful, and forthright. We turned him loose on the case, and when he was all done interviewing all the witnesses, it was his conclusion that the charges never should have been filed against our client.

The first task of our private investigator was to dig up the criminal records, if any, of the potential Commonwealth witnesses. We already discussed the Mayfair record. Normally, only *crimen falsi* (crimes in which the principal element is that of dishonesty) offenses are admissible to impeach a witness. The bad check case may qualify. One other exception would be if the claim is self-defense and the witness has a history of aggression. The harassment may qualify here.

Both were borderline. I would argue strongly that these cases were admissible for their appropriate purposes with the weight of their evidence to be given due consideration by the jury. In other words, we would argue that this evidence should not be set aside before the jury even heard of the crimes—let the jury hear it and give it its due weight.

One of Mayfair's backups was Devon McGee, a punk who carried quite a bit of baggage for the prosecution. He was already a convict: a theft conviction in November of 2005 filed by the Mercer, PA, police, a Criminal Mischief/ theft conviction in the same month, and a marijuana case filed by the State Police in 2006. As the Williams case was pending (June 25, 2007), McGee was arrested and charged by the Grove City Police with furnishing alcohol to an eight-year-old child. Mom must be very proud.

McGee was on paper at the time the three boys showed up on the Williams' porch. Usually someone of McGee's caliber is given one chance at probation before a Common Pleas Judge, and if this opportunity is butchered, prison is eminent. Mayfair's buddy had every reason to play ball with the prosecution, and as a prosecution witness would be a nice piece of meat for us to chew up at the trial. I was actually concerned that the Commonwealth might not call him as a witness to bolster Mayfair's testimony.

The other backup for Mayfair was a juvenile. Legally still an infant, he would not have had the opportunity, as of yet, to develop a criminal record. But Cody and his mother would both testify that this was a big, ugly kid that in no way looked under eighteen years of age. He was standing on the bottom of their porch steps reeking of alcohol and smoking a cigarette.

Next the private investigator reviewed the Police Reports and Investigation and tore it to shreds. The police only interviewed the victim and his two buddies. Mr. Graham interviewed several others who had evidence that

Mayfair had pre-planned the assault on Williams, and when he saw Williams emerge with the gun, he tried to seize it from Williams right before the shot. It would be important as to the distance the shot was fired from the victim in this case, or any case, and the clothing of the victim would contain physical evidence that would assist in making this determination. None of this evidence was gathered or documented. Several other areas of the Police Investigation were weak. We had plenty of ammunition to attack the decision of the police to prosecute Williams. The self-righteous police, instead of backtracking and filling in their missing evidence, would attempt to tear down our investigation and witnesses. This is often a successful strategy of prosecutors and is a good reason why many defense attorneys simply refuse to present a defense or call witnesses.

We showed up for the Pre-Trial Conference and the jurors were ready to be *voir dired*, or questioned under oath, regarding their knowledge of the case and/or any predispositions they may have. When we explained our defense, the trial judge told us that based upon Mr. Williams' testimony that he broke free from Mayfair, then entered the house and emerged with a gun that was later fired, he may not receive the benefit of a self-defense instruction to the jury. I was flabbergasted at this but had to discuss the possibility with Mr. Williams before he made a concrete decision. In the meantime, and before the Judge made his off-the-cuff "ruling," the Commonwealth had offered a plea bargain. Mr. Williams would plead guilty to the felony aggravated assault but the government would not invoke the mandatory five-year sentence nor any deadly weapon enhancements. Thus, the prosecution was leaving it up to the Judge as to an appropriate sentence.

Normally, this is a good thing. Although neither side is always tickled with a Judge's sentence, and a convicted defendant almost never breaks into applause after being sentenced, leaving the ultimate sentencing decision in the hands of the trial judge generates the best and fairest result almost every time.

It is important to note that in a criminal case, the jury has no idea whether or not a mandatory sentence is involved. It is improper to even mention the sentencing phase of the case to the jury, since the penalty imposed is in the sole province of the court (subject to wide legislative invasions, as we are discussing). Therefore, a jury makes its decision blind to the existence of any mandatory sentences, guidelines, or enhancement. The only exception to this rule is that juries do decide in a small percentage of homicide cases whether or not the convicted murderer receives life imprisonment or death.

The problem in this case was that the mandatory sentence of five years in a state penitentiary warped the result. In this, and every other case where a mandatory sentence is in the game, the result is warped. Cody Williams would not be good state penitentiary material, and we suspected that the trial judge knew that and would not sentence him "to the state." This meant a sentence in jail of one year or less. If we went to trial and did not even get the opportunity to present a defense of justification, a conviction was likely. And the five-year mandatory sentence would be back in the mix, like an invasive cancer, crowding out the discretion of the sentencing judge, eating the flesh away from rationality, decency, and common sense. The legislative invasion of the judiciary poisons the system, so Cody Williams took the plea and became a criminal.

After his sentencing on November 3, 2008, Cody became a yardbird. The Felony-1 Aggravated Assault he was convicted of carried an offense gravity score of eleven on a scale of one to thirteen. His prior record score was zero. The standard range under the PA Sentencing Guidelines is thirty-six to fifty-four months minimum with a mitigated minimum of twenty-four months and an aggravated minimum of sixty-six months. This meant that he could face a minimum of two to five and a half years with a maximum term of at least double the minimum. The Judge gave Cody eighteen to forty-two months, which was below the mitigated range due to his imperfect self-defense or provocation, his poor health, and his cooperation with the local police in other matters. This meant a state sentence, though, since the maximum was twenty-four months or greater.

Here we have a first-time offender who was assaulted on his own porch by a stranger plus two backup hoods under cover of darkness, a timid youth with debilitating physical problems, who in a panic fired a gun at his attacker, and who winds up in a state prison specifically because the trigger of a mandatory sentence was cocked on his head throughout the process. And although the sentencing statistics will not show that a mandatory sentence was imposed in this case, it was the controlling factor from beginning to end.

This type of case is not at all unusual. In fact, it is quite common. I can guarantee that this type of case is pending before the courts on a daily basis across the country. And on a daily basis justice is perverted in this same way by the legislative branch of government. Often, innocent people are forced to plead guilty and go to prison to avoid the risk of prodigious mandatory state prison sentences. Guilty people are forced to go to trial if the District Attorney does not waive the mandatory prison sentence applicable to the case because they have nothing to lose and they occasionally are acquitted by juries. Results are not only imperfect; they are terrible. The end result of mandatory sentences is the swelling of our already bloated prison population and diminished faith in our judicial system. The result is injustice. It is Yardbird USA.

# CHAPTER 15

# Say Good Bye To Mandatory Prison Sentences And Guidelines

The only way to reverse the prison population explosion in this country is to displace the legislature and its bureaucratic mechanisms out of the courtroom where it never should have been in the first place.

Mandatory prison sentences and sentence "guidelines" set forth by the Legislative branches should have been struck down as unconstitutional right off the bat. They violate the separation of powers by dictating how the judicial branch operates in one of its most important functions, the disposition of criminal offenders.

The politics of sentencing has taken over where common sense and good judgment should operate. Being "tough on crime" is a wonderful way to get votes, grab a seat in the legislature, and stay in power. Nearly everyone has been the victim of a crime. Crime is a serious problem. Being tough on criminals means putting them behind bars to keep the public safe. Who can possibly argue with this? And legislators can point to specific bills they have sponsored or voted for to prove that they are "tough on crime," whether it be more and more mandatory sentences, "three strikes you're out," or other similar measures.

But these laws have clearly infringed upon the judiciary's province.

■

Why The Judge?

The Sentencing Judge in a criminal case has often times heard a trial in which all of the relevant and important evidence surrounding the case has been presented by both sides. The Judge has had an opportunity to observe the Defendant throughout the proceedings. The Judge has heard the jury's verdict and often times has spoken to members of the jury after the trial. The Judge has received feedback from his tipstaffs, his law clerk, and other courtroom personnel. If there has been a plea instead of a trial, the Judge has heard the evidence at the plea hearing surrounding the offense. He knows why the plea was entered and why other charges may be dismissed.

After the verdict or plea, the Judge has access to a Victim Impact Statement, where the victim provides the Court with a statement on how the crime has affected him or her, what it has cost and what is involved for restitution. That is, if there is a victim. Thousands of people are in jails across the country having committed a crime in which the victim is listed as "society." This would be the case in all drug or paraphernalia possession charges and in a vast majority of driving under the influence charges where there is no accident. Unfortunately, many of these offenses come with mandatory imprisonment dictated by the legislature.

A Pre-Sentence report is done where the defendant's entire past is revealed. The Judge knows whether the defendant is bi-polar or whether he is an alcoholic or drug addict. The Judge knows whether the defendant has been a victim of sexual abuse in the past. The Judge knows whether the defendant has a normal upbringing or whether he came from a broken family or some other tragic background, or whether he has squandered opportunities and second chances in the past.

The Judge knows the Defendant's age and the victim's age. He knows their educational background. The Judge knows the entire criminal record of the Defendant and how she has responded to probation or other supervision in the past.

The Judge has an opportunity to hear from the prosecutor as to their position on the offense and any witnesses can be called by the prosecutor to support his position at the sentence hearing. The family of a victim killed by a driver negligently running a stop sign may testify the devastating impact of their loss. The family may show forgiveness and ask for mercy or may beg the Judge for maximum retribution. The Judge observes this testimony and takes it in.

The Defendant has the right to allocution, or to testify and speak to the Sentencing Judge. She can explain how her drug addiction, which led to her running off the road and killing a man who was servicing his truck on an exit ramp, has changed her life; how she has successfully completed rehab, has found faith in God, and is now helping others overcome addiction; how she has turned around her life and is now helping other people. She can call witnesses that testify to her metamorphosis; the addictions counselor that supervised her healing, felt her remorse, and how the Defendant has actually helped others overcome addiction.

The Judge is in position to determine whether the offender is likely to repeat—whether the situation giving rise to the crime is likely to recur or not. This is one of the most important factors in sentencing. Many defendants have already paid for their crime before they come before the Judge for sentencing. They have paid for a lawyer (unless indigent); they have suffered public humiliation with their name in the paper. They may have spent time in jail already until making bail. Many have lost jobs, alienated family and friends, and lost property and possessions. If there is a victim, the Defendant by law must pay back any damage done by way of restitution. On top of all this, the government must make its statement by punishing the Defendant, and now the Judge must follow guidelines and sometimes mandatory sentences set forth by politicians who know absolutely none of the things just outlined above.

■

Why Not Politicians?

The Order imposing a sentence is called a "Judgment of Sentence." Who is in a better position to make a Judgment of Sentence on a convicted individual, the Judge who has all of the information outlined above or a legislator? A man who has to answer to the electorate, the defense bar, and the district attorney's office, or a car dealer that has just been elected to office? This elected representative may never have read the Constitution or studied law. But to trumpet the sound of "tough on crime" is a no-brainer and the herd instinct bowls over common sense.

This is all to be expected. The politico does what the majority will approve of. If we have ten people in a room and isolate a person who inherited one million dollars from an aunt, and ask them to vote on whether 10 percent of his inherited money should be donated towards world peace and hunger prevention, the vote will be 9-1 in favor of the redistribution. And the politico will pass the law for which the majority booms.

But this is a deprivation of property without due process of law and it is an unconstitutional taking, i.e. theft. If such a law was passed, it is up to the judiciary to strike it down as unconstitutional. The JUDICIARY is present to PROTECT THE RIGHTS OF THE MINORITY.

Jack W. Cline

The authors of the Constitution, James Madison and Alexander Hamilton, recognized the Judiciary as the last defense: "The courts of justice are to be considered as the bulwarks of a limited Constitution against legislative encroachments."[21] Two important conclusions follow from this. First, judicial offices should be of permanent tenure to preserve "that independent spirit in the judges which must be essential to the faithful performance of so arduous a duty"[22]. Periodic appointments and popular elections involving judges would be "fatal to their necessary independence and create too great a disposition to consult popularity to justify a reliance that nothing would be consulted but the Constitution and the laws[23].

The Judiciary is present to protect the rights of the losers, the despised, the gay, the dim, the bi-polar, the compulsive gambler, the kleptomaniac, the ugly, and all miscreants that our society produces. Madison stated: "It is easy to see that it would require an uncommon portion of fortitude in the judges to do their duty as faithful guardians of the Constitution, where legislative invasion of it had been initiated by the major voice of the community"[24]. Indeed, no other branch of the government has the ability or the duty to insure that these interests are protected to the same degree as the interests of the Warren Buffetts, the Jimmy Buffetts, and the O.J. Simpsons and the Bart Simpsons.

Why, then, did the Judiciary drop the ball so disastrously when confronted with the issue of mandatory sentences and sentence guidelines? The courts obviously eschewed this "uncommon portion of fortitude," as we see in the Geneva Spells case (Chapter 16), and became cow-

---

21 Rossiter, Clinton, *The Federalist Papers,* Hamilton, Madison, Jay, Mentor 1961, p. 469.
22 Id.
23 Id., at 471.
24 Id., at 470.

ards. And the clear reason for this is our deviation from the teachings of Madison and Hamilton when we allow Judges to be elected to terms (in Pennsylvania) rather than being afforded lifetime tenures.

■

Mandatory means arbitrary. Sentences dictated by the legislatures as posturing "tough on crime" agendas create some absurd results. In Pennsylvania now there are several mandatory sentences imposed in drug trafficking crimes. If Stella Strungout has been caught with possession of, say, roxys by the local police, she is often given a choice of making a controlled "buy" from someone a little higher up in the drug food chain for a shot at leniency when she is sentenced. Stella Strungout becomes Stella Snitch. In this situation all kinds of machinations go on with a drug task force and local police, including surveillance, marking bills, searches of the snitch, laboratory testing. No expense seems to be spared. Stella begs her supplier to meet her so she can buy more dope. The duped supplier succumbs and meets Stella in a Wal-Mart parking lot where she pays $240 for eight roxys (a Schedule II narcotic). The duped supplier is caught with the marked money and Stella Snitch has the roxys for the lab to test. But rather than make an immediate arrest, a few more controlled buys are set up. Then the accused is faced with several charges.

Eight roxys would typically weigh about two grams. Two grams multiplied by fourteen equals one ounce. Two grams multiplied by 225 is still less than a pound! The street value of the pills could actually be less than the cost of a ticket to a Pittsburgh Penguins hockey game and would account for only .000025 per cent of the cost of the Arlen Specter Memorial Library.

Yet, incredibly, each of these offenses carries a mandatory minimum sentence of two years imprisonment.

Moreover, if there are multiple convictions, the mandatory sentence of imprisonment increases to three years minimum and a $10,000 fine. It would not be uncommon for a pedestrian street dealer in this scenario to be facing three separate counts on controlled buys, leaving he or she exposed to nine years' minimum state penitentiary service, paid for by the taxpayers of Pennsylvania.

While it is hard to feel sorry for a convicted drug dealer who is headed for the hoosegow, it is not hard to feel sorry for the taxpayers. The consensus is that the cost to room and board a yardbird is somewhere around $40,000 per year, and I suspect that this is grossly understated when all the collateral expenses are figured in. Shamefully, the taxpayers are getting nothing for this money. Drug trafficking has increased markedly over the past several years instead of being eliminated. Where one dealer is taken off the street, another one steps in. Use and addiction is at an all-time high. The war on drugs has been a colossal failure to society and the mandatory sentence laws have perverted the justice system by politicizing it. Obsequious courts have failed to stand their ground and have allowed these laws to pass constitutional standards.

We discuss the Pennsylvania budget for 2010 in Chapter 17 (Prison Is A Drag). That budget teaches us why we cannot rely on politicians to make the correct choices on crime and punishment. While the budget whacked $7 million from the Pennsylvania State Police, politicos committed $10 million for the Arlen Specter library near the Philadelphia University! This senseless expenditure edifying the pompous ex-Senator from Pennsylvania, who switches political parties depending upon wind direction, was matched by another $10 million pork project known as the John P. Murtha Center for Public Policy. The Murtha ten million expands on the previous government construction of a worthless airport near decrepit Johnstown,

PA. "Twenty million to erect monuments to these pork-barrel politicians is really a slap in the face," said Matthew Brouillette, president of the Commonwealth Foundation, a Harrisburg think tank critical of the RACP program.[25]

The Federal Prison Scheme is even worse than that of the states. Ninety-seven percent of Federal Criminal Defendants face sentencing and 80 percent receive a prison term. Alan Ellis, Esq. and Michael Henderson have written a 580-page book titled *Favorable Prison Guidebook,* which advises lawyers on the placement and sentencing guidance applicable to all prisons and a detailed description of the attributes and offerings of each of the 105 federal prisons. It is subtitled: "How to ensure that your client gets into the best possible prison and is released at the earliest opportunity" (James Publishing, 2010). The mere need for this book among federal criminal law practitioners speaks volumes.

Was it a Pyrrhic victory for the Feds and State Legislatures to enact mandatory sentences and sentencing guidelines? Have these politically motivated weapons against crime, shoved down the throats of an unexplainably pussified judiciary, now become the petard of our system? If so, is it then time for the Judiciary to relinquish its role as the weak sister in this dangerous and expensive game?

---

25 See "Specter Library Aid Draws Criticism," by Robert Swift, Harrisburg Bureau Chief. Read more: http://thetimes-tribune.com/news/specter-library-aid-draws-criticism.

# CHAPTER 16

# Geneva Spells and the Pansyfied Judiciary

L et us fathom in amazement the case of the *Common-wealth of Pennsylvania vs. Geneva Spells*[26]. If we can, it will be no mystery as to why Pennsylvania ranks first among all the states in gathering up and incarcerating human beings behind bars. Years after this decision, which has never been over ruled, Pennsylvania continues to gain in prison population while other states are beginning to see the light and shed prisoners, albeit for wrongheaded and dangerous reasons.

In 2008-2009, six states reduced their prison population by at least one thousand persons. Twenty-four states continued to fatten up their prison populations, but none as efficiently as Pennsylvania, which added another 2,122 yardbirds, by far the largest increase of any state for the year 2008-2009. The Keystone State of self-righteous Puritans increased its jailed citizenry by the same amount as Maine, North Dakota, South Dakota, Kansas, Vermont, Idaho, Tennessee, Minnesota, New Mexico, Alaska, Oregon, Washington, and West Virginia combined, with another 131 prisoners to spare. We have an outgoing gover-

---

26 612 A.2d 458 (Pa. Super. 1992)

nor who views prison costs as a "sacred cow" in the budget and a governor elect (Tom Corbett) who seeks to address prisons and crime without any input from the defense lawyers' association (PACDL) that has wrestled with these issues on a daily basis since the prison population explosion began some thirty years ago. (Governor Elect Thomas Corbett's "Transition Team for Criminal Justice Issues" did not contain any members of the Public Defenders Association nor the private defense bar! It was initially only comprised of prosecution-related entities and agencies. This does not portend a balanced approach to dealing with crime or prison population explosion but may predict only an acceleration of our current woes).

Pennsylvania has achieved this growth in prison population despite a declining and eldern population. Florida, with a growing population (and many being illegal immigrants), simply could not keep up with the rabid pace of Pennsylvania, adding only 1,527 prisoners. A close third was Indiana with 1,496.[27]

How can Pennsylvania do it? *Commonwealth v. Spells* illustrates.

On September 18, 1987, Geneva Spells purchased a gun in Dallas, Texas where she lived, and she flew to Philadelphia to shoot her estranged husband. Finding her husband at work, she walked up to him and, from a distance of one foot, pulled the trigger of the loaded gun pointed directly at his head. The estranged husband avoided death because the gun had a very tight trigger, which the defendant could not operate. When the gun did not go off, she repeatedly pulled the trigger to discharge the gun. Security guards took the weapon from the defendant and arrested her. That same day she described the incident as follows: "I pointed it at him and pulled the trigger as hard as I could, but it did not go

---

27 The Pew Center on the States, April 2010.

off. I kept pulling the trigger, and then he took it from me. I did this because of past problems over the past twenty-one years. The way I feel right now, I would do it again, and the next time I will take the time to do it more properly"[28]. (You cannot make this stuff up.)

It was an open and shut case of attempted murder. An attempt to commit murder requires a specific intent to kill and can only constitute an attempt to commit murder of the *first* degree. [Second and third degree murder are unintended results of a specific intent to commit a felony or serious bodily harm, not to kill. [*Commonwealth v. Griffin*, 456 A.2d 171, 177 (Pa.Super. 1983)]. Attempted murder is rated as an offense gravity score of thirteen (on a scale of one to fourteen) where no serious bodily injury occurs.

But Ms. Spells was not charged with attempted murder. She was charged with the lesser-included offense of aggravated assault: an attempt to cause serious bodily harm [18 Pa.C.S.A. Section 2702(a)(1)]. Aggravated assault, attempting to cause serious bodily injury, is rated as on offense gravity score of ten out of fourteen where no serious bodily injury occurs.

Why did the government charge her with the lesser crime of aggravated assault rather than attempted homicide, which the defendant essentially confessed to? Perhaps because the aggravated assault charge contained a five- to ten-year mandatory minimum sentence due to the involvement of a deadly weapon [42 Pa.C.S. A. Section 9712(a)], whereas the attempted homicide charge inexplicably contained no such deadly weapon enhancement even when a deadly weapon was used!

The first mistake made by defense counsel was to take a trial by judge rather than a trial by jury. Ms. Spells was summarily convicted by the court after hearing the

28 Id., at 459-460.

stipulated testimony. A jury, however, may have nullified such a verdict. The alleged confession could have been questioned. The shenanigans of the prosecution in not charging her with what she should have been charged with (attempted murder vs. aggravated assault), sympathy for an abused wife who suffered from "battered wife syndrome," or based upon other intangible factors.

Recall the O.J. Simpson murder trial. The jury acquitted an obviously guilty Simpson due to prosecutorial idiocies—trying on the glove that did not fit and clear planting of evidence by imbecilic police. Simpson's blood allegedly found *on the victim's sock* at the crime scene was later proven to contain EDTA, an additive used in forensic blood type testing, which proved even more interesting in that 1.5 ml of Simpson's blood sample had mysteriously disappeared while in police custody.[29] The evidence "plant" backfired.

Juries sometimes find defendant's not guilty even when they have committed the crime if the cheating by police is flagrant enough. A jury trial should never be waived, especially in the face of such serious charges and when there is absolutely no injury to the victim. When there is a mandatory sentence applicable and thus nothing to lose, the right to a trial by jury should never, ever be waived.

The second mistake made by Spells was to allow her fate to be placed into the cowardly hands of a Pennsylvania Appellate Court. Spells's counsel challenged the mandatory five-year sentence eloquently, stating, "Is not a mandatory five-year to ten-year sentence of incarceration for aggravated assault unlawful, as it is unconstitutionally disproportionate and irrational when aggravated assault is a lesser included offense of attempted murder of the first degree, a crime for which there is no mandatory sentence?"[30]. Spells's

---

29 *Bodies of Evidence*, Brian Innes, pp. 13-15, Amber Books Ltd., 2000.
30 Spells at 459.

counsel also pointed out the anomaly created by the mandatory sentence muddle: "The Commonwealth's constitutional
obligation to prove the commission of offenses beyond a
reasonable doubt is fatally eviscerated if the Commonwealth
can chose to prove less (aggravated assault) and be resulted
by obtaining more—here a mandatory sentence"[31].

The Superior Court stated to the second argument: "We
are not persuaded. The charging function is totally with the
district attorney, both initially and as to which charges to
pursue"[32].

As to the first question, the court also showed its pol-
troonery. The Superior Court of Pennsylvania would not
disturb or even question the five-year mandatory state prison
sentence even though this was a perfect opportunity to do so.
It was an ideal time to strike down the legislatively mandated
and inappropriate sentence, given that there was no injury
sustained in the case and the government deliberately failed
to charge the defendant with the crime she confessed to in
order to invoke the mandatory sentence on a lesser charge!
On the contrary, the Superior Court stated that "reviewing
courts . . . should grant substantial deference to the broad
authority that legislatures necessarily possess in determining
the types and limits of punishments for crimes"[33]

What? We are to give deference to a legislature that
clearly omitted attempted homicide from the deadly
weapon provisions of section 9712 and placed a lesser
offense above it on a penalty scale? On the very same page
that the quote from Justice Kennedy appears in the Spells

31 Id., at 465.
32 Id., at 465.
33 Id., at 462, parroting a United States Supreme Court opinion by Justice Kennedy,
who "finds even less discretion in reviewing a sentence for proportionality when a
mandatory sentence is involved. *To set aside petitioner's mandatory sentence would
require rejection not of the judgment of a single jurist, as in Solem, but rather the
collective wisdom of the Michigan Legislature and, as a consequence, the Michigan
citizenry.*" [Harmelin, 111 S.Ct. at 2708, fn 10, Id., at 463, 464. (Italics mine).

opinion, the Spells opinion also acknowledges this wild incongruence, yet ignores and fails to remedy the legislative bungle, stating: "The facts of the present case include the visible use of a firearm; clearly, but for this legislative omission, section 9712 would be applicable under the facts of this case. Surely, an argument cannot be made that an attempted murder by use of a firearm should be treated differently than other crimes committed with firearms"[34]. And in a concurring opinion, Justice Wieand feebly noted, "I am also unable to discern the legislature's logic in imposing a mandatory minimum sentence for visibly possessing a firearm during the commission of an aggravated assault, while not imposing a mandatory minimum sentence for the visible possession of a firearm during an attempted murder. Perhaps it would be advisable for the legislature to reevaluate the grading scheme for the offenses of aggravated assault and attempted murder, as well as the exclusion of attempted murder from the purview of the mandatory minimum sentencing provisions."[35]

Thus we see how carefully and prudently the legislature proceeds when enacting mandatory sentence provisions that can put people behind bars for years and years. And we see how the judicial pansies in our appellate courts have countenanced this tragedy.

In Spells, the Superior court also put its rubber stamp on previous rulings that upheld challenges to the mandatory sentences set by the legislature, stating that section 9712 does not violate the prohibition against cruel and unusual punishment, does not violate equal protection, and does not unconstitutionally deny substantive due process by requiring proof of visible possession of a weapon to be made by a preponderance of evidence.[36]

34 Id., at 464, p. 12.
35 Id., at 465.
36 Id., at 462.

Jack W. Cline

This court should have strung up the Legislature by its collective testes. This court held the perfect opportunity to wreck the whole stinking scheme of mandatory sentences. Instead the self-gelded court politely criticized a gross error and obvious injustice, sanctified the basic rationale of the mandatory sentencing scheme, and sent Ms. Spells away for five years minimum to a state penitentiary.

# CHAPTER 17

# Todd Fergus:
# The Kid Rapist and the
# Sentencing Guideline Absurdity

The purpose of sentencing guidelines are purportedly to aid the courts in imposing uniform sentences for offenses classified in like manner. Each offense is given an "Offense Gravity Score" ranging from fourteen—most serious—to one—least serious. Each defendant has a "Prior Record Score" where his prior criminal record is charted and classified from zero to five. There are enhancements for repeat felony offenders and repeat violent offenders. The Offense Gravity Score is shown on the "Y" axis and the Prior Record Score is shown on the "X" axis. Where the two numbers meet is a square on the chart, which magically renders the range of the minimum sentence to be imposed. At the far right of the chart is an "Aggravated/Mitigated" number, which allows the court to add or subtract a number of months based upon statutorily designated factors. In truth, it does add some amount of discretion into the

---

Based upon the cases of *Commonwealth vs. RBF* No. 1127 Crim. 2010 (Mercer County, Pennsylvania) and *Commonwealth of Pennsylvania vs. BMM* No. 04-1004 (Butler County, Pennsylvania)

sentence without forcing a Sentencing Court to go outside the guideline matrix.

But the guidelines are at once worthless and goofy.

To illustrate their worthlessness, we need only look at one very common scenario under the guidelines. A defendant has no prior record score (meaning he has no previous felonies and less than two misdemeanors in the past ten years). He has committed a Level 2 offense with an offense gravity score of five. This is a common result in the system as OGS=5 covers all the way from Felony 2 Burglary down to DUI (second offense; highest BAC rate or refusal of chemical test) along with most theft and drug delivery offenses. What is the magical minimum sentence result that the District Attorney and the Defense Attorney can tell the defendant to expect if he is convicted or enters a plea of guilty to an offense in this category? The "guideline" result is zero to nine months, plus or minus three months. In other words, the Judge is within the guidelines if he does not impose one minute of jail time all the way up to imposition of a one-year minimum (State Penitentiary Sentence). In most real-life scenarios, the guidelines are just about that useless.

■

### *Commonwealth v. Todd Fergus*

To illustrate their goofiness, consider the case of Todd Fergus. Todd grew up in Butler, PA. He was born on October 2, 1991. Todd was a lanky redhead just out of acne and braces. He was a baby-faced, skinny, young man that did not look as if he had ever shaved. He hung with a tough crowd and was out of school working for his father in a specialty vehicle decal paint shop just outside of town.

Brittany was also from Butler. She was born on October 27, 1995. Todd and Brittany grew up together in the neighborhood. Brittany's older brother and Todd were great friends and played on the same ball team and went to the same church. Brittany always liked Todd and when she reached puberty at age twelve, Todd was all she could think about. The puppy love crush had turned to lust.

Todd, by then, was already in high school and was about to get his driver's license. But as time sped along, Brittany became a well-nourished and aggressive young lady and directed her insatiable hormonal impulses towards Todd. When she was fourteen and he was eighteen, they went to a birthday party at a mutual friend's house and found themselves in the back seat of a Chevy Malibu. They did some smooching and light petting and Brittany took off her panties. She unbuckled Todd's pants and pulled them down. Todd was lying peacefully on his back, but he had begun to feel erectile tissues engorge his penis. Brittany then mounted Todd and was ready to embark in all-out sexual intercourse with the elder teen. But Todd was able to resist, thinking maturely and responsibly of the risk of pregnancy for the younger teen and STD for himself. But he was still hot and horny, so he penetrated the rabid Brittany digitally while she utilized her hands on his aroused organ. Nothing more came of the encounter as they were busted by friends.

The two met again at another party. In the basement of their house, with another adolescent couple half-engaged, Todd and Brittany made out again. They ended up on the floor beneath a dusty old sofa and participated in an act of dry coitus. During or after that maneuver, they again stimu-lated each other's private areas digitally. Todd refused for a second time to fornicate.

Brittany's parents caught wind of the activities from a friend of Brittany, who also had the hots for Todd. The rumors were running as wild as the estrogen, and Mom and Dad questioned Brittany, believing that she had been violated and perhaps impregnated. She denied the fornication but was forced to concede the digital activity. Because her private area was sore, either from the strong fingers of Todd or from abrading zippers between the dry copulation, Brittany's parents would have none of it. A physician could make no weight of the contention that Brittany had lost her virginity, but Mom and Dad, quite embarrassed, went to the local police.

The police took a written statement from Brittany where she acknowledged only the digital penetration. The police then asked to question Todd (now eighteen and an adult) and his parents went to the station with him where Todd confessed his being an adolescent. He denied intercourse but accepted full responsibility for the penetration by digit of the young and fevered Brittany. The police consulted with the Office of the District Attorney, who advised charges of Aggravated Indecent Assault under section 3125 of the Crimes Code (of Pennsylvania).

This section reads: "A person commits a felony of the second degree (Aggravated Indecent Assault) when the person engages in penetration, however slight, of the genitals or anus of a complainant with a part of the person's body for any purpose other than good faith medical, hygienic or law enforcement procedures: mother is less than 13 years of age. There are several sub-sections applicable. To commit this crime the defendant must have done it:(1 or 2) without the complainant's consent or by forcible compulsion (this would not apply since the contact was consensual), (3) by threat of forcible compulsion that would prevent resistance by a person of reasonable resolution (again, not applicable, since no threat was needed); (4) who is unconscious or where the person knows that the complainant is unaware that the sexual intercourse is occurring (was not alleged here by the complainant so not applicable); (5) where the person has substantially impaired the complainant's power to appraise or control his or her conduct by administering or employing, without the knowledge of the complainant, drugs, intoxicants, or other means for the purpose of preventing resistance (factually inapplicable to Brittany and Todd's unadulterated encounter); (6) who suffers from a mental disability which renders him or her incapable of consent (getting closer); (7) The Complainant is less than thirteen years of age (Brittany was fourteen) ; or (8) the complainant is less than sixteen years of age and the person is four or more years older than the complainant and the complainant and person are not married to each other (BINGO!). Todd was four years and twenty-five days older than the fully developed Brittany, though he actually looked the same age, if not slightly younger.

Aggravated Indecent Assault is a felony of the second degree punishable by a maximum term of imprisonment of ten years [18 Pa.C.S.A. Section 3106(b)(3)]. More significantly, it rates as a ten on the Offense Gravity Score under the Sentencing Guidelines (204 Pa. Code Section 303.15). An OGS of ten is a "Level 5" offense, the highest level offense on the chart, calling for State Incarceration even with no prior record whatsoever. An offense gravity score of ten puts the crime of Todd Fergus at the same level as Kidnapping, Aggravated Assault, (attempting serious bodily injury), Arson (with a person inside the structure burnt down), Homicide by Vehicle while Driving Under the Influence( in a work zone), and Delivery of (50 to 100 grams) of Controlled Substance (cocaine). The Standard Range Sentence with no prior record for Aggravated Indecent Assault is twenty-two to thirty-six months incarceration plus or minus twelve months, in other words ten to forty-eight months, and almost a guaranteed trip to a state penitentiary.

Now let's assume that Todd had yielded unto the animal passions of the aggressive and single-minded young lady when they were in the back seat of that car. Not being sexually active, he is unprepared for the climactic event and fails to generate a condom. Todd completes the act of sexual intercourse with Brittany riveted on top of him, and he quickly ejaculates inside her womb. Another teenage pregnancy is precipitated. Poor Todd and his family thought Mom and Dad were angry before—now they are enraged and out for blood—and support money.

What crime has Todd committed here? It is not statutory rape because Brittany is above the protected age (thirteen) for that crime. Todd has committed "Statutory Sexual Assault" under section 3122.1 of the Crimes Code, which reads: "A person commits a felony of the second degree when that person engages in sexual intercourse with a complainant under the age of sixteen years and that person is four or more years older than the complainant and the complainant and the person are not married to each other."

As stated, Statutory Sexual Assault is a Felony of the Second Degree, the same as Aggravated Indecent Assault. However, on the sentencing guidelines, it rates as a seven, substantially lower than the crime that does not involve intercourse but only heavy petting! An OGS of seven is a "Level 3" offense calling for State/County Incarceration with eligibility for Restrictive Intermediate Punishment. It is on a level with such offenses as Robbery (inflicting or threatening serious bodily harm), Burglary (of a home with no one present), Theft (of $50,000 to $100,000), Identity Theft (third offense) and Delivery of Cocaine (less than 2.5 grams). The standard range sentence with no prior record for Statutory Sexual Assault is six to fourteen months incarceration, plus or minus six months, i.e. zero to twenty months. This is an utterly worthless guideline for one with zero prior record score.

It is not difficult to argue the absurdity of the guidelines in this situation. And although the facts of this case are somewhat unusual, the basic scenario is not. Statutory sexual assault is meant to protect young teens from the overwhelming advances of mature perverts, not teenagers just a few days past the statutory cut off. Yet the guidelines treat these two offenders the same.

More imbecilic is the sentencing guidelines' comparison between the statutory sexual assault (OGS=7) and the aggravated indecent assault (OGS=10). The message to our youth is to keep your hands and lips off a young lady's genitalia. If you are going to get caught, better to fornicate.

This case and many others like it is pure proof that offenses cannot be molded into cookie cutter dies and assigned numbers to categorize them. There will always be incongruities and absurdities that translate to unfair and unjust results. There simply is no normal case.

These unique and difficult issues cannot be handled from the halls of state or federal legislatures where common sense is usually checked in at the coat-racks. These important and real issues profoundly influencing people's lives must be handled on the spot by the lawyers involved, and ultimately decided by a Judge.

# CHAPTER 18

# Prison Is A Drag

Can you imagine a more profound economic drag on a society than that of its prison system? It is a system of double damnation. We are paying Peter to watch Paul. We are paying police, prosecutors, judges, sheriffs, jail guards, probation and parole officers, house arrest coordinators, *and all their staffs* to confine and control the lives of an astoundingly large and growing percentage of our population. The taxpayers, out of their own work and incomes, ultimately roll over and pay for these services. We misemploy resources and manpower to detain other citizens, depriving them of an opportunity or the ability to lead productive lives, at least while they are incarcerated. While in prison, a person is a complete ward of the state, just as a monkey in a zoo, and all the resources delineated below are used to keep him or her that way.

At the top of the next page is a chart showing the expenditures on these public services in the United States of America. It is obvious how the expenditures have exploded. Figures are in billions of dollars: (Bureau of Justice Statistics).

In twenty-five years covered by this study, "Police" expenditures improved more than five-fold, "Judicial" expenditures blossomed six fold, and "Correction" Expenditures, being confined to prison expenses alone, ejaculated—from 9 to almost 70 billion dollars!—nearly an eight

| Year | Police Expenditures | Judicial Expenditures | Correction Expenditures |
|------|---------------------|------------------------|--------------------------|
| 1982 | 19.0 | 7.8 | 9.0 |
| 1986 | 26.3 | 11.5 | 15.8 |
| 1992 | 41.3 | 20.9 | 31.5 |
| 1996 | 53.0 | 26.2 | 41.0 |
| 2002 | 79.5 | 40.4 | 59.6 |
| 2006 | 98.8 | 46.9 | 68.7 |

fold redoubling doubling. If this trend would continue, we would spend twice as much on corrections by 2030 ($560 billion) than we spent on World War II ($288 Billion).[37]

To put these figures in some perspective, imagine what the entire US Government expenditures were in 1971; all the social welfare expenditures, military expenditures—including winding up a war in Vietnam, space exploration, energy and education, social security, roads, bridges, government employees—everything spent by the federal government. That figure was $210.172 billion (OMB 2004 Budget Historical Tables). Now look at the above figures. Adding the police, judicial, and correction expenditures, representing our cost of detaining and imprisoning our own people, we spent $214.4 billion. Incredibly, we spent more on the prison system in 2006 than the entire United States government spent in 1971.

We could go on and on with these astounding statistics and anyone interested further can simply obtain more figures from reliable Internet sources. I can guarantee you the pattern will be consistent and with no exceptions. No one can argue the fact that we are world-renowned experts in throwing money at a system designed to imprison our own population. We are truly Yardbird USA.

---

37 Calore, Paul, "What World War II Cost the United States," *What It Costs*, LLC 2011.

The economic effect of this policy cannot be underestimated. Please bear in mind that while we are throwing money at prisons, paying sheriffs, turnkeys at the jails, probation and parole officers, and all the others associated with the prison system, either directly or indirectly; we are taking these people away from private sector employment where they could be contributing productive resources to the economy. And by paying them to hold down millions of our citizenry, we ensure that the imprisoned sector of the populace can contribute absolutely nothing to the productive end of the economy, save the occasional prison-crafted license plate.

It is truly the zero sum scenario—the prisoners digging the ditch and the corrections personnel filling it up, while both unwittingly pound lumps on the taxpayers.

Many states are beginning to feel this crunch, Pennsylvania being one of them. California is facing a budget crisis and has acknowledged that the prison situation is playing a significant role. Corrections officers working overtime are raking in taxpayer monies at astounding rates, some going over the $100,000 per year mark. I know emergency room physicians who handle thousands of patients a year and administer an entire staff of personnel who make less money than this. And I know lawyers who battle for the rights of the weak, oppressed, and mentally ill on a daily basis who make far less. Jail turnkeys hauling in six figures a year for work that may be potentially dangerous, but is mostly mindless and boring, is another signal that we are upside down.

California could have saved some money by screening its jail turnkeys a little closer. Imperial County is defending lawsuits from prisoners who have alleged that various jail guards have forced them into unwanted sexual activities. In a case that simply could not be made up, one prisoner alleged that a guard, CD, forced oral sex from a prisoner who was in an observation cell following a suicide attempt [*Fernandez v. Morris*, USDC (SD Cal) Case No. 3.2008-cv-00601-H-CAB and Flores-Nunez. Dillon, USDC (SD Cal) Case No. 3.2008-cv-01881-W-CAB]. How the guards figured that they could avoid detection for forced cunnilingus/fellatio in an observation cell will be a mystery that is unlikely to be resolved, at least in this particular study.

Pennsylvania is considering and has already enacted laws that would purportedly slow down the growth of the prison population by taking such measures as reducing technical parole violators' incarceration, allowing early parole even in state cases, and giving sentencing judges more discretion. State Intermediate Punishment Programs that usher drug and alcohol offenders from the jails to rehab to halfway houses generate statistical improvements, but they are not the answer to the problem. They are simply band-aids that create more and more layers of very expensive bureaucracy. (The 2011-1012 Pennsylvania budget allocates over thirty million dollars of expense to probation, parole and intermediate punishment.)

As one of our former Judges in Mercer County used to state to defendants in sentence court who begged for community service in lieu of imprisonment: "I'm not going to sentence you to community service. If I order you to rake leaves, then I have to hire someone to watch you." This is where we are headed with the new legislative band-aids.

But we are in a situation now where the legislature is dictating who will and will not serve jail time on the back end, just as the legislature dictated who will be serving jail on the front end by criminalizing practically every offensive act known to man and enacting mandatory sentencing, enhancements, and guidelines. The legislators created this profound problem to begin with and should not be trusted with resolving it. In fact, it is the worst scenario possible, the legislature and not the judiciary determining who will be incarcerated and who will not.

We need less legislation, not more. Rather than piling on more and more laws, regulations, guidelines, and other such bureaucratic pish posh, we need to eliminate the flab in the current system by repealing laws that have not worked. We need to repeal laws providing mandatory sentences and sentencing guidelines and turn back sentencing decisions to the judiciary. If the legislatures do not have the stones to give up their unearned powers over court room proceedings, which I suspect they do not, then the courts need to take control again by holding that mandatory sentencing usurps the judicial function and strike down such laws as unconstitutional. This must be done both at the state and federal level.

More laws governing the release of prisoners controlled by politicians are not the answer to the problem, while on paper it may assuage the current prison population explosion. Politicians must step out of the arena and allow the courts to operate their system, which is imperfect in many respects, but in all respects superior to the intermeddling of politicos.

■

Governor Ed Rendell speaks eloquently out of both sides of his mouth. After a parolee shot a Philadelphia Police Officer in late 2008, Governor Rendell grandstanded with a decree that stopped all paroles for two months for a "review of the system." Mark Bergstrom, the Executive Director of the State Commission on Sentencing, opined, "The decision not to parole people for a couple months really did back up people in the state's system, and I think we're still seeing the results of that moratorium today." The Parole Board says its operations have mostly returned to normal. But even without last year's spike, Pennsylvania faces a stubborn long-term trend: In 1980 the state housed about eight thousand inmates. Now that number is more than fifty thousand.[38]

In 2010 the budget for corrections, including federal aid, was increased by $81.6 million dollars to a total of $1.87 billion. This budget compares to $453 million in 1994, an increase of 412.8 percent over that time period! The cost for corrections expenditures now exceeds higher education expenses for the fourteen state universities for the first time ever, and as a budgetary category, expenditures for corrections is surpassed only by the budget for public schools ($5.8 billion) (*The Patriot News*, July 1, 2010). It is important to bear in mind that this does not include the costs of corrections each county incurs, nor federal correction expenditures, all of which have headed in the same direction as Pennsylvania.

Rendell mopes that he cannot do anything about correction costs since it involves public safety, for which the state is mandated to pay. This is, of course, a political cop-out. The last time I checked, the Governor in the Commonwealth of Pennsylvania still had veto power. He could have vetoed the approval to build four prisons in 2010 to be completed by 2013 at a cost to the taxpayers of over $800 million. That may force the state to do something else with the 2,100 inmates shipped to prisons in Michigan and Virginia, with Pennsylvania bearing the costs. These state prisons will be full the minute they are opened, based on current demographics.

Pennsylvania, as well as many other states, is heading for fiscal crises. The Pennsylvania budget defers payments for many pork projects, pensions, and corrections to later years and wistfully counts upon federal aid to a much

---

38 From PA Prisons Growing More Than Most, Monday, March 29, 2010, Tom Dreisbach, PSEA Website.

greater extent than necessary. While state budget fallouts are beyond the scope of this discussion, they are indirectly related to the criminal justice system because cuts in that area are likely to again impinge upon the role of the judiciary on its own playing field.

State budget crises usually lead to cries for help from the Federal Government. States cannot print money but the Federal Government has this insidious prerogative. The U.S. can print dollars and grant them to the various states foundering in debt, but such grants necessarily come with strings attached. This process gradually shifts power from the states to the federal government as an unanticipated consequence. Pennsylvania already has 80 percent of its spending mandated by the Federal Government. This power exerted by the Federal Government over the states cannot be overestimated. It derogates the delicate balance of power the Constitution directed and creates another warp in the system.

To be fair, Fast Eddie Rendell inherited the "tough on crime" regime of Pennsylvania Governor Thomas "Rocky" Ridge, previous Pennsylvania Governor from Erie, PA. Rocky Ridge was a fourth-rate District Attorney from Erie County who developed considerable political skills. He touted mandatory and three-strike sentences and presided over the construction of new prison facilities and other programs, which engorged the prison population and ratcheted in budgetary increases in corrections for years to come. After terming out as Governor of Pennsylvania, Rocky Ridge had a short stint as director of homeland security and has since thankfully resigned into political obscurity.

It appears that Fast Eddie had seen the light—too late—and his Executive Budget Address commented on the sorry state of Prison population and the associated costs:

"The proposed FY2010-2011 budget also provides for substantial increases in our Correction costs. I am troubled by this increase, and I know that many of you share this concern. We have worked together on critical reforms over the years, yet the cost of housing prisoners in Pennsylvania continues to rise. We must reverse this trend, if for no other reason than the failure to do so threatens to overwhelm our ability to meet skyrocketing prison costs. Increased funding for public education is one great way to address this problem, because it provides an opportunity for our young people to choose the right path. But we must do more to reduce the rising costs of incarceration, and I welcome the opportunity to partner with you to achieve this goal" (Executive Budget Address, Fiscal Year 2010-2011, Edward G. Rendell, Governor, February 9, 2010).

Education is certainly an important component to the solution, but the Governor has not been in the trenches of the criminal justice system. The significant redneck population, by definition, abhors and runs from education of any sort, and is proud to distain any effort to be educated. Education simply cannot be shoved down the throats of the rednecks, nor anyone else for that matter. Joe Six Pack has no interest whatsoever in learning the intricacies of the Pythagorean Theorem or Belgian History when there is a tree stand to erect for hunting deer or a NASCAR pileup on TV.

Moreover, many of the younger criminal set, particularly with drug crimes, are already educated. The proliferation of drugs and other mind-altering substances used by young people must be a reflection of the despair and hopelessness they perceive. The political process has created a future of enormous debt, decrepit cities (Detroit, Cleveland, Philadelphia and many others, mostly in the Northeast), and lost opportunity as jobs go overseas and the cost of higher education soars out of reach.

In addition, many of the older criminal set are long past hope and care of being educated. But courts can and do order defendants of all ages to complete vocational training or attain GED if they are not high school graduates. There is a modicum of success shown in these programs, depending upon the individual. Again, these matters are best left to the Court and not to the Legislature.

An alternative suggestion to force-fed education would be to institute a thorough study of the sociological patterns of some other civilized, or uncivilized, nations in history, such as Red China, aboriginal Australia or the likes of Libya. All of these societies have had comparably modest prison populations. Perhaps we could glean what aspects of the behavior of their citizenry could be easily mimicked here in the United States of America to help us overcome our prison fetish.

Unfortunately there is no simple or obvious solution. But having been in the trenches of the criminal justice system on a daily basis for a quarter century, I can easily tell what is NOT the correct answer, and that is more legislation, more bureaucracy, more control by the political branch. My thesis throughout this tome has been to identify the problem, and that is clearly political hijacking of the judicial process by the Legislative branch. Perhaps just by eliminating or reducing the input from this branch of our government will in and of itself yield positive results.

The great blowhard, Rendell, certainly hit the right notes in his speech. The task will now be for politicians to pay more than lip service to this immense economic problem and to create a non-political solution, returning the sentencing aspect of the criminal justice system to the courts. And the task for the courts will be to stop cowering before legislative skullduggery and do the right thing when the opportunity arises.

# CHAPTER 19

# Nikita Needs a Lawyer

With the United States running away with the title of the World's Most Proliferate Jailer, defense lawyers should be ashamed. Despite all our work and effort, we lead the world in futility as our clients are by far the most likely to end up in the hoosegow. The defense bar has to take some responsibility for Yardbird USA. It is no surprise that we have very little lobbying power in the legislatures for advancing the rights of criminals, and the legislature has warped the playing field accordingly. But too many weak and rotten cases filed by the government go without vigorous defenses. It becomes easier to plea bargain for lower charges, particularly with defendants that do not have the money for a competent and vigorous defense or who are sitting in jail racking up time served because they could not post bail under our present system.

The role of the defense lawyer is critical to balance the power in our system, which is weighted heavier and heavier on the side of the government as time goes on. The defense lawyer should be proud of his or her role. Gerry Spence and Alan Dershowitz eloquently set forth the critical and noble role played by the defense bar in far more

*Commonwealth v. NLD* Cr 580-2010 (Venango County)

eloquent fashion than I could. I would highly recommend their works, particularly Spence's *Give Me Liberty: Freeing Ourselves in the Twenty-First Century,* and Dershowitz's *The Best Defense.*

Cops and even prosecutors occasionally look at me with disdain and ask how I can represent the guilty, the scum, the trash and other "worthless" people. I often reply to such self righteous twerps that I do not take on the lives and values of my clients any more than a pediatrician or a psychiatrist takes on the life and role of his patients. I tell them my role is to stop the likes of you from running roughshod over an accused; to make your job in depriving someone of their liberty as difficult as possible; to insure that you have not cut corners, acted with prejudice or malice, and that you have not violated our constitution to secure evidence. I tell them that we are a part of the process, and without us, you would have no peace or security against the weight of the government.

Truth be told, there is some redeeming characteristic in nearly every person we represent, and we serve our clients better by finding that positive quality. I was almost frightened to meet Nikita, given what I had read about her. Yet she turned out to be one of the most respectful, pleasant, honest, and appreciative people I have ever met.

■

Nikita Daniels was born on November 20, 1980, just a few days after Ronald Reagan annihilated Jimmy Carter in the presidential election. Her mother had been injured badly in a motor vehicle accident and was totally disabled, so Nikita had a chance to run as a young lady, and she took advantage of that opportunity.

Nikita got into the alcohol and drugs at a young age and suffered with occasional bouts of exhibitionism. But she had her share of problems that may not have been directly related to substance abuse. She is diagnosed with bi-polar and schizoaffective disorder and is prescribed some powerful meds to allay the symptoms. On the day of the incident, she was on prescribed Wellbrutrin, Prozac, and Neurotin. The panic attacks have produced disability checks of $600 per month.

She was known, without any prompting and despite much discouragement from her peers and others, to climb up atop bars without any clothing on her and boogie away. At 5'2" and 220 pounds, it must have been quite frightening to both patrons and management.

Despite some unusual characteristics, Nikita appeared to be a harmless and pleasant young lady lacking self-esteem, by no means intentionally a criminal.

However, she was on parole from an Aggravated Assault while Driving Under the Influence in 2004 in Mercer County, and she had just obtained her driver's license back in March 2010. This was concomitant with a trip to Warren State Psychiatric Hospital after a breakup with a boyfriend.

On June 11, 2010, Nikita met a Grace Lindsey for no good reason and they headed to a bar in Stoneboro, Pennsylvania. Nikita was driving her Grand Am. They hung out at the bar, had a few drinks, and discovered from someone there named "Woodsy" that there was a bonfire up around Utica, PA, between Stoneboro and Franklin where Mercer and Venango County intersect, and where deer and bear outnumber men and women with high school diplomas. The closest road was Buttermilk Hill Road, and Grace and Nikita followed Woodsy and some others to get there. They arrived at about midnight on June 12.

Grace said that she had "a beer" but Nikita had some beers and swallowed a few shots from a bottle of liquor. Nikita had to "go to the bathroom" and asked Grace to accompany her. The bathroom was on open-air design at the edge of the field behind the car. Next Nikita locked her keys in the car along with Grace's purse, which contained important Oxycontin and Vicoden pills.

According to Grace, Nikita suddenly began acting "delusional." She was babbling, yelling, and making no sense at all. Grace got a beer bottle from the party and, with the permission of Nikita, smashed the passenger side window to reach in and obtain the keys. Grace received a cut on her thumb as a result of her heroics. Then, all of a sudden, Nikita ripped off her sundress and got naked. She began hugging one of the male hosts and Grace had never been so embarrassed in all her life. She made a monumental decision that it was time to go.

One of the guys backed Nikita's car out of the tight parking space and Grace got in the driver's seat to drive the drunken Nikita out of the area. Nikita, still naked, got in the passenger seat and off they went. But the journey was a short one. According to Grace, Nikita grabbed the wheel of the car and started shaking it. Grace could not control the vehicle; she bailed out. She remembered to grab her purse with her drugs in it, and she grabbed Nikita's cell phone, and she got out of the vehicle and began to walk. She left the keys in the car for Nikita. According to Grace, Nikita tried to run her over and then peeled out of the private party, driving her Grand Am in an unknown direction.

At 3:13 a.m. on the same day, Tom Cutchall, who resided on a quiet, dead-end street in Franklin, Pennsylvania, heard a knock on his door. He was somewhat perplexed at this, but when he saw Nikita Daniels at his door, he was extraordinarily perplexed. Nikita had no clothing on and invited herself into the house. Mr. Cutchall did not think that was a good idea. Out in his front yard was the Grand Am, stuck on an embankment. He called 911.

When the police arrived, they noted the presence of a stuporously intoxicated young lady named Nikita Daniels. The police asked some basic questions to Nikita, which were answered much the same way a person suffering from senile dementia and recovering from a potent anesthesia might answer, if they had also just taken in a bottle of whiskey. Ms. Daniels made no sense. She said she was "just driving home" but she lived twenty-seven miles away in Mercer. She said she was with "Shena," then it was "Tony," and then it was "Terri," then "Tony." Adorning her hair was a combination of sticks, leaves, and twigs from trees behind Cutchall's house; she was still naked and could have cared less. She was in no shape to perform any field sobriety tests or even to be a subject of the "drug recognition" tests performed by certain "qualified" state policemen. She could not even stand without assistance.

The vehicle was almost immediately towed from the scene before police made any investigation regarding its condition or contents. There was no inventory search of the vehicle, which would have shown the presence of a Diet Pepsi and a fruit beverage, both freshly purchased and resting in the console. There was blood on the steering wheel and throughout the driver's compartment of the vehicle, none of which was documented by the police. The passenger window was broken out.

Nikita was arrested for DUI by the Franklin Police. There are three counts of DUI pending, all Misdemeanors (M-1) carrying mandatory jail time of ninety days up to five years. The counts are based upon Driving Under the Influence of (1) Alcohol, (2) Drugs, and (3) Combination of Alcohol and Drugs. The open lewdness charge is a Misdemeanor- 3 charge, akin to a disorderly conduct, false registration of a domestic animal, or fortune telling.

The scene of the accident in Franklin was about nine miles from the Buttermilk Hill Road bonfire. For reasons never explained to date, Grace Lindsey made a call to the Franklin Police department to ask if they had found Nikita Daniels' vehicle. Grace made a big fuss about how drunk

Nikita was and that Nikita gave Grace permission to break the passenger window to get the keys. Although Grace made these calls with Nikita's cell phone from the Stoneboro tower, there were several previous calls made from the same cell phone, which came from the Franklin tower.

Nikita tested positive for alcohol at a whopping .257 percent, more than three times the legal limit. She also tested positive for Propoxyphene and Norpropoxyphene, which are found in Oxycontin. She could have no more steered her vehicle from the Buttermilk Hill Road bonfire nine country miles to Franklin than she could have written one of Chopin's Piano Concerto's or landed a space shuttle on Jupiter.

I began to question Grace on her story. At the preliminary hearing, Grace went on about the bizarre behavior of Nikita. It turns out that a "Tony" had to help her into the passenger seat of her own vehicle, that she could not even stand on her own, and that she was hanging on to "Tony." Grace drove out of the bonfire but Nikita had grabbed the wheel and Grace was not about to put herself in danger. She got out and walked down an unknown road and was almost run over. I asked her why, when she got out, did she not take the keys, and she said, "It's her (Nikita's) vehicle."

Grace's story began to unravel. She claimed that she tried to walk back to the bonfire, just a few hundred yards and one turn away, but could not find it. However, under a stroke of unbelievable luck, two guys in a truck saw her, picked her up, and drove her back to her house in Fredonia, some twenty-five miles away. She did not remember their names and did not have their phone numbers.

After her arrest by the Franklin Police, Ms. Daniels was taken into custody at the Cambridge Springs State Correctional facility on July 16, 2010 where she remained until her "max date" of November 27, 2010 as an alleged parole violator. Her incarceration was automatic under Pennsylvania law, as it was based on a detainer for arrest on new criminal charges. She would have to sit in jail until either her acquittal or her max date on parole.

If she is acquitted of these pending DUI charges, she will have endured 132 days of unwarranted jail time, and if convicted she may have already overstayed her welcome as a yardbird.

The case against Nikita for Driving Under the Influence seemed to rest heavily upon the testimony of Grace Lindsey, since the police responding to the accident scene never saw Nikita driving, and in actuality, had no idea in the world who was driving the car. The police felt her story was important enough that they asked her to come in and make a written statement affirming that which she had told them over the phone. This tactic has a twofold purpose. First, it pins down the witness to her story. If she tries to change it or back down from it, she can be confronted with the written statement by the cops and threatened with "false statements to law enforcement personnel," a criminal offense. Second, it relieves the police of investigating the incident any further. They can rely on this statement and file the charges. If the story later proves to be absurd, so be it.

The police did no investigation whatsoever. They rested on the fact that Nikita was found near her car and that she was drunk. It is not a crime, however, to be drunk near a vehicle, at least not at the point of this writing, although the legislatures are always busy. Under the present state of the law, there must be proof of operating the vehicle. Only Grace Lindsey could testify to this.

Nikita Daniels had no recollection of the evening from the point in which she was assisted into the passenger side of her vehicle when they left the Buttermilk Hill Road bonfire until she was aroused in the hospital and told she had wrecked her car in Franklin. Nikita was convinced there was no way she could have possibly driven her vehicle, naked, from the Bonfire at Buttermilk Hill all the way to

Franklin in her profoundly inebriated condition. She was kept in the hospital for observation for two nights. Unfortunately, Nikita was of no use in piecing together the events of this bizarre morning, so we hired our private investigator to work on the case.

Our investigation team, Ross-Graham, interviewed Mr. Cutchall, the victim of the mid-morning surprise exposure. Incredibly, he stated without equivocation that he heard two different female voices arguing outside that night before the knock on the door, lending credence to the theory that there was someone else in the vehicle. He also said he told the police this, but apparently such important evidence complicated the situation too much for them.

Mr. Graham also discovered the phone calls made by Grace from Nikita's phone came off the Franklin cell tower, which may also have included Buttermilk Hill Road, but these cell phone calls were also consistent with her being in Franklin in the wee hours of the morn. The two soft drinks in the console were circumstantial evidence of two people in the vehicle. The blood, mostly on the driver's side and steering wheel, was consistent with Grace Lindsey being there, not Nikita, who was not cut.

Grace Lindsey's fortuitous hitchhike from Buttermilk Hill Road all the way to Fredonia would be about a forty-five-minute drive through twisting roads, halfway across the county of Mercer. There were apparently firemen from the Utica Volunteer Fire Department at the scene of the bonfire at some time that night responding to an emergency of some sort, but the chief of the UVFD assured Mr. Graham that no one from the fire department would have given Grace Lindsey a ride across the county to her apartment in Fredonia, even if she were injured.

Who was this Grace Lindsey? I felt it was important to make a thorough background check on her. I would do this in any case, but all the more so when I felt (a) there was some reason for a witness to fabricate, and (b) the story being offered up did not make any sense. I was not disappointed or surprised with the results of the search.

Grace Lindsey was a small-town gal from Fredonia, Pennsylvania (population 502). At age 19, she embarked on a journey through the criminal justice system in whirlwind fashion. On September 1, 2006, she was guilty of underage drinking in Stoneboro, Pennsylvania (population 1052) (NT 574-2006 District Court 35-3-02). Within seventy-two hours, the police were at her service again, this time on a charge of Defiant Trespass, which she pleaded guilty to on September 8, 2006 (NT 573-2006 District Court 35-3-02). On September 17, 2006, just nine days later, she was arrested and charged with two counts of Driving Under The Influence, Underage Drinking, DUI by a Minor, Driving an Unregistered Vehicle, Driving a Vehicle Without Insurance, along with three other vehicle code violations. She pleaded guilty to DUI and operating with no insurance (No. 1931 Crim. 2006, Mercer County). Apparently undaunted by the DUI and other drinking charges, Lindsey was arrested for Underage Drinking again as well as Public Drunkenness and pleaded guilty to the whole of them on November 20, 2006 (NT 564 and 565-2006 District Court 28-3-03).

Around the Yuletide season of that same year, young Lindsey busied herself shopping in the Meadville area. She visited at least six retail establishments and obtained her Christmas gifts at all of them. Apparently, however, Lindsey neglected to pay for those items taken from the retail establishments, resulting in six retail theft charges being filed on January 23, 2007. Lindsey was guilty of each and every charge (NT 30, 31, 32, 33, 34, 35-2007 District Court 30-3-02).

On September 29, 2008, Lindsey was charged with Felony-2 Retail Theft, which was later reduced to Misdemeanor-1 Retail Theft, to which she pleaded guilty (No. 357 Crim. 2008, Mercer County).

In 2010 Lindsey mixed the offenses she was charged with nicely. She also achieved some success in court as the local magistrates were apparently getting weary of trying to collect money from her. Charges of Harassment were filed and withdrawn in April (NT 253-2010 District Court 35-3-02). Another Harassment charge was dismissed in July of 2010 (NT 337-2010 District Court 35-3-01). A Felony-3 Retail Theft was inexplicably withdrawn in October 2010. (NT 751-2010 District Court 35-2-02), but that could be refilled any time within the next five years.

But Lindsey was by no means batting 1,000 percent. Also in 2010, Lindsey was charged with Theft by Deception-False Impression, Conspiracy to Commit Theft by Deception-False Impression, Possession of Instruments of Crime with Intent to Use, and Retail Theft. These charges are pending (No. 1715 Crim. 2010, Mercer County). She was also charged in 2010 with a Felony-3 Count of Retail Theft, and this charge is also pending (No. 1856 Crim. 2010, Mercer County). She took a summer break from the felonies and misdemeanor charges and mixed in a charge of Driving an Unregistered Vehicle in McKeesport, PA, on August 19. She was found guilty of this charge after a trial (TR 1399-2010 District Court 5-2-13). Finally, In August 2010, Lindsey was found guilty of Driving While Operating Privilege was Suspended (TR 1935-2010 District Court 35-3-02). It is important to note that this charge carried with it an automatic one-year license suspension, to be added on to any existing suspensions.

Just before the pages turned on 2010, before she could enact her 2011 New Year's resolutions, Grace Lindsey was arrested again, on December 29, 2010. This time Lindsey upped the ante substantially: seven felony counts of Retail Theft; three Counts of Theft by Deception (M-1); three counts of receiving stolen property (M-1); three counts of Theft by Deception (M-2); and three counts of receiving stolen property (M-2) (No. 201 Crim. 2011, Mercer County).

Armed with the testimony of this witness, the Commonwealth plowed forward with its DUI case, blind to any concept that their star witness was a thief, drunk, and a liar or that there may, in fact, be a defense to the charges.

Some things are never going to change. Lazy police and Lazy District Attorneys are two of them. It is painful, however, to see lazy defense lawyers, especially when they have the opportunity to pounce on the government's weak or rotten cases. I can state one thing for sure: if Nikita Daniels is guilty of any offense in this case, it will not be because she pleaded guilty.

Moreover, it is simply wrong that innocent people sit in jails unless and until competent defenders have an opportunity to try their cases. And once again, if bail were required to be paid by the government, the pain and injustice would be alleviated.

The same would hold true for a detainer. Nikita was an alleged parole violator. Her intoxication that night may well be a technical parole violation leading to some sanction by the court, but the new criminal charges of DUI and open lewdness, both quite serious, triggered the detainer which landed her in jail. As discussed in the Zimburger case, such a result eviscerates the presumption of innocence. No detainer should ever be honored from a parole officer. A Judge should only order a detainer after a hearing in which there is proof of a new crime and proof that conviction of this crime would likely result in further incarceration, a much tougher standard than the present. Procedurally, this would not be difficult as the Judge need only review the testimony of the preliminary hearing and any evidence the defense wished to present.

Nikita Daniels is scheduled for trial in June 2011. And if Ms. Daniels were exonerated of these charges, she would have been falsely imprisoned for over four months. Under our current system, who is to answer to her for that?

# CHAPTER 20

# Jay Negra Fights A Two Front War

As more and more individuals are released from prison, the ranks of those on parole will continue to swell. The government exercises unfettered control over the billowing crowd of people on probation and parole. (See page xix.) This creates a serious issue with personal liberty as most states allow probation and parole officers to incarcerate their subjects with the stroke of the pen or, more frequently, a phone call. As we have discussed, this "detainer" acts as a "NO BAIL" order pending resolution of alleged offenses and it is obnoxious to the concept of the presumption of innocence.

The same day that I was contacted to represent a parole agent charged with his second DUI and possession of marijuana, I received a call from a fevered mother of a former client. Her son had just been incarcerated by a parole agent in Mercer County on a detainer for new charges that were nothing less than freakish.

On June 12, 2011, a sixteen-year-old girl who had spent much of the last year hospitalized for psychiatric care inexplicably reported a crime (by way of her RCF Crime Victim Center counselor) to the local police department. She

---

Mercer County, PA Cases 1780 Cr 2008 and 858 Cr. 2011)

claimed that she was with her boyfriend "Shooter" back on February 18, and they wanted to have sex. "Shooter" was twenty-two and they weren't sure of the legalities of fornicating, so "Shooter" placed a call to the State Police. The police noted the ages of the players and sanctified the event, first asking "Shooter" if she was "hot." "Pretty good looking," retorted "Shooter." "Then go ahead and 'hit' her" encouraged the good cop. The two amateurs then had clumsy sex, which was supposedly recorded on the cell phone camera of Jay Negra, a cousin of "Shooter."

Later testimony regarding the phone taping of the sex revealed that the 15-30 second video was of inferior quality and it was impossible to identify the faces of the actors. It was also taken at very close range, with only orifices showing on the recording, making this amateur porn production almost indistinguishable from a video of baboons breeding in the dark. The video was never even transferred to a card for permanent display, and was deleted at the request of the girl, according to her own testimony. What could have just remained a forgetful evening for three stoned idiots was, however, transformed into a nightmare for all of us by the government. This effort was propelled by the RCF Crime Victim Center Counselor and later handed off to local borough Patrolman Matt Lewellen.

But how the young girl could quite grasp what was happening is a questionable feat in itself. She was not too bright to begin with and suffered from depression, anxiety attacks, and PTSD (Post Traumatic Stress Disorder). She was on three strong medications—Vyvanse, Paxil, and Seroquel. (These meds were later changed to Wellbutrin, Prozac, Abilify, and Concerta, which she was taking at the time of her testimony in June). Prior to fornicating with "Shooter" she had also ingested beer, marijuana, and K-2, a new and readily available get-high substance found in corner delis and filling stations. This was clearly a messed up young lassie.

"Shooter" was also messed up in many ways. He was smoking pot and drinking, and most likely doing his share of K-2. "Shooter" was notorious in the area and had compiled quite a criminal record for such a young punk. His convictions included defiant trespassing #1 (District Court 35-3-02; NT 160-2003), defiant trespassing #2 (District Court 35-3-02; NT 462-2006), purchasing alcohol as a minor (District Court 35-3-02; NT 540-2007), Selling or furnishing liquor to a minor, Possession of a controlled substance, and Driving while operating privilege is suspended (Mercer County CR 1286- 2008). Attempted Burglary charges were dropped in exchange for a plea to Criminal Attempt to Criminal Trespass (a Felony-3) (Mercer County CR 1725-2009). A Felony-1 Burglary charge stuck in 2010 which resulted in a six to twenty-three month jail sentence. (Mercer County CR 91-2010). There is a bit more. Retail theft charges were strong enough to result in a guilty plea on June 28, 2009 (District Court 35-3-02; NT 368-2009). Attempted Burglary charges are pending (at District Court 35-3-02; CR 232-2009). Felony charges of Manufacture, Delivery or Possession with intent to manufacture or deliver controlled substances and two counts of corruption of minors pending in Mercer County, Pennsylvania, a hotbed for yardbirds, at Mercer County CR 557-2011. "Shooter" was digging a bigger and bigger hole for himself. Talking to snitches in the prison, he may have seized upon the idea that dragging his cousin into the dirt with him may actually help him out of his double felony hole.

Based upon this story told by "Shooter" and his young lover on June 11, this Matt Lewellen, a borough patrolman, filed serious criminal charges against Jay Negra for an event unreported for nearly four months. Charges filed against Jay were Sexual Abuse of Children-Depicting child performing sex act on computer (Felony-2), Corruption of Minors (Felony-3) and Child Pornography (Felony-3). The patrolman who solved this mysterious and important crime and who swore out the affidavit of probable cause against Jay Negra was a convicted criminal himself. Lewellen had been found guilty of False Statements to Obtain U.C. Benefits under Title 43 Section 871(A) of Pennsylvania Statutes. (MDJ 05-2-47 PC 416-09). This crime is a classic "crimen falsi" offense which can be used to impeach the veracity of the witness (here the police officer himself) as being a dishonest individual. The jury or judge deciding the case may justifiably use the dishonesty-based criminal conviction when assessing the credibility of the witness.

This is a scenario that we will begin to encounter more and more, as a higher and higher percentage of our people serve time for criminal offenses. More and more cases will involve convicts testifying against each other and against those not yet behind bars. It is an ugly thought for defense lawyers and prosecutors alike.

Jay faced a potential jail sentence of twenty-four years plus the revocation of his parole and loss of street time.

As stated, his parole officer immediately issued a detainer, which was followed up by the Judge's Detention Order on June 22, 2011. These are perfunctory machinations. Any new criminal allegation, no matter how farcical, lands a probationer or parolee in the hoosegow. Jay's bail was set at $10,000, also a joke, but it made no difference because the detainer would keep him behind bars even if he was bailed out.

An obvious slime-ball and a teenager whose brain must resemble a burnt scrambled egg have combined with a story so stupid that it may have been impossible to make up. If the story is false, Jay Negra sits in jail as a yardbird unjustly. If it is true, he sits in jail as a yardbird unjustly. A man or woman in this country should sit in jail only after he or she is convicted, and after a sentence hearing giving due weight to all the circumstances involved. It is possible that he sits in jail so long, awaiting trial on the new charges, that he is backed into accepting a plea bargain to an offense giving him time served as his sentence. If he chooses to exercise his right to a trial on the charges pending, he will be threatened with this: "If you go down on the three felony convictions, we will recommend state time."

Here, the hammer of the detainer, issued by a lowly parole agent, warps the playing field so perversely that it is nothing less than shameful. The inordinate power afforded to probation officers and parole agents by the legislatures has been a large contributor to Yardbird USA.

Parole and probation officers have no business filling up our prisons. At this point in time they are more powerful than police and equal with Judges with regard to parole/probation detention. Given time, they will surpass the immense power already prescribed to game wardens, deputy sheriffs, national park security guards, IRS field agents, liquor store inspectors, parking meter maids, airport security scanners, and dog catchers. It is not as free and easy to live in these United States as may have been envisioned by Jefferson or Madison.

# Conclusion

The United States of America has a fetish for incarceration, and has become by far and away the world's most prolific jailer. The cost and drag of creating and maintaining the world's greatest prison system should not be underestimated. The economic effect is profound. Although it is difficult to accurately assemble and categorize all public costs and expenditures, it is reasonably safe to state that prisons ("corrections") are the fourth greatest public expenditure in this country, behind only defense, welfare, and education.

The flaccid courts have acquiesced to the invasion of the criminal justice system by politicians, who look good and righteous when enacting mandatory sentences, guidelines and a "war on drugs." These interfering factors have all backfired and continue to warp the playing field and mete out injustices. The judiciary must regain control of the criminal justice system. Substantial chunks of lard must be cut out of the crimes code.

The present bail scheme requiring defendants to post bail, the amount of which is dictated by the government, renders the presumption of innocence a joke.

Finally, the prison is a walled ghetto. It should be inflicted upon our fellow man only as a last resort, much as the skunk only reluctantly sprays the putrid acetate thioesters from its anal glands.

The criminal justice system is the means by which the government deprives its own citizens of life and liberty. Such a momentous role must not be left to politicians.

Time will prove or disprove this case. If the illustrations, opinions, and warnings herein appear to be absurdly obvious ten or fifteen or twenty years down the road, then that in and of itself will be enough sanctification.

On the other hand, if I have erred, there will still be something learned from it all—I will have qualified myself for political office of some sort.

CPSIA information can be obtained at www.ICGtesting.com
Printed in the USA
BVOW01s1527211214

379909BV00002B/8/P